R60-00

D1239887

FLOORS

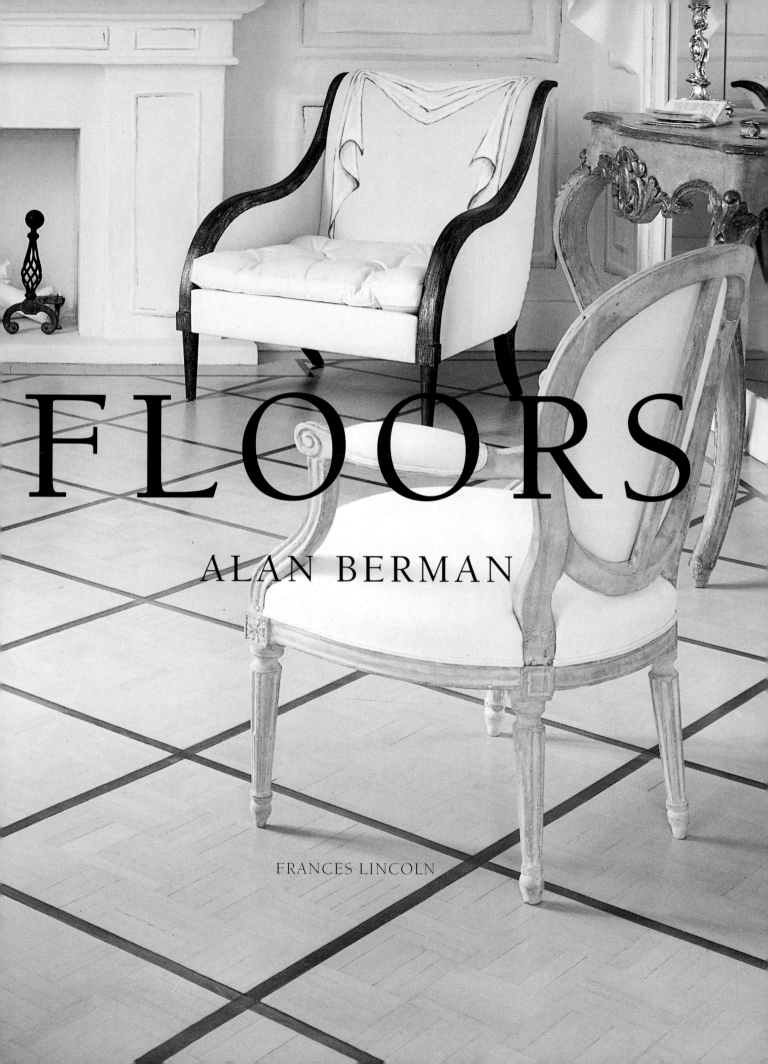

FLOORS

ALAN BERMAN

FRANCES LINCOLN

Charles and Sadie:
thank you

Frances Lincoln Limited
4 Torriano Mews, Torriano Avenue
London NW5 2RZ

First Frances Lincoln edition 1997

British Library Cataloguing-in-Publication Data
A catalogue record for this book is available from the
British Library

ISBN 0-7112-1062-4

Set in Berkeley Book and Berkeley by Frances Lincoln Limited
Printed in Hong Kong by Kwong Fat Offset Printing Co. Ltd

2 4 6 8 9 7 5 3

HALF TITLE PAGE *This sanded and sealed woodblock epitomizes the best and most beautiful but undemonstrative and timeless floor that will suit any furnishing style. The strong grain is endlessly satisfying, the colour is rich and quiet, and the high-gloss polish gives fascinating plays of light.*

FRONTISPIECE *The predominant cream tone of this painted parquet floor is alleviated by the crisp contrast of the dark bands which echoes the same balanced contrast of large areas of light and dark linear elements in the furniture.*

OPPOSITE *Modern encaustic tiles provide a graphic counterpoint to their plain surroundings. They can be used as separate inserts and to form continuous borders.*

CONTENTS

THE POTENTIAL OF FLOORS

People have long transformed the ground on which they tread into the stuff of dreams. In our imagination paradise is paved with gold, and to recreate that sense of opulence we strew herbs before kings and rose petals before brides, and we roll out the red carpet for special occasions. But the magic of floors lies not only in their ability to suggest beauty. By introducing changes to the surface and delineating boundaries through differences in pattern and texture, we can imbue certain areas with particular significance, as a child's chalk circle establishes a special domain. Floors also have the power to influence, even to create, the feeling of a room through their appeal to the senses. The echoing sound of a footfall on stone, the warm softness of carpet, the scent of wood and polish, the nuances of colour, light and pattern – all contribute to our perception of internal spaces.

In addition to their physical characteristics, different materials carry cultural resonances. The cool luxury of marble is associated with Renaissance palaces; simple chequerboards of tiles suggest the calm of seventeenth-century Dutch interiors; colourful Eastern rugs conjure images of nomadic people, whose floors had of necessity to be portable. The subtlety of tatami mats on wood in traditional Japanese houses or the rich honesty of well-scrubbed Shaker boards demonstrate that there can be a positive virtue in investing in the best possible floor and little else. A fine floor, well made from the best-quality materials, can be an heirloom in itself and is perhaps all a room requires. Yet, in our utilitarian age, when form has followed function and regard has generally been paid only to maintenance and practicality, the potential magic of floors has largely been ignored until quite recently, except by the serious professional designer.

There is no reason, however, why anyone should not be able to create beautiful and practical floors for their home. It goes without saying that flooring or reflooring are major undertakings and, unless money is no object and you have somewhere else to live during the process, you are unlikely to contemplate such a step very often. So it is all the more important to define your wants and needs carefully from the outset, and to stimulate your imagination by examining as many other floors as possible. Avoid being a slave to fashion and simply copying something that works elsewhere. Perhaps more than any other surface area, the floors will set the style and atmosphere of your home. Colourful or muted, solid or yielding, they form an integral part of your interior design and can express both your own personality and the nature of the room in which they are laid, from the strictly utilitarian to the luxurious.

This book attempts to review the magic and potential of floors; to discuss the many design issues involved and how these work; and to explore the range of different materials available, their practical characteristics, their origins and traditional uses, and the principles of installation and maintenance. The practical relationship of the floor to other elements of the building, such as heating and insulating against sound and damp, is also considered. Appreciating the infinite riches of flooring and understanding the materials and techniques involved should help you not only to enjoy floors but to transform the surface beneath your feet into a delight that will give pleasure for years to come.

Choosing Floors

The choice of floor should be so well suited to the space, its use and its qualities that it will accommodate future changes in the more superficial elements of any decorating scheme. Rooms which grow and develop organically with alterations in taste, family size or use will always feel the most comfortable and inviting, and the most personal. Selecting floors for different parts of the house will present you with a bewildering number of practical points to consider. How will the room be used? How easy will the floor be to clean? How hard-wearing will it be? How will it fit into the existing structure and into your decorating scheme? Many of the demands you make of your floor will contradict each other, so it may be helpful to list your priorities and keep them to hand when faced with seductive samples in the showroom. White tiles may offer just the look you want, but every dirty mark will have to be washed off them immediately to keep their original pristine appearance. Brick is wonderfully tough and rustic to the eye but hardly suitable if there will be children playing on the floor. Think through every aspect of the room and the way you will be using it. The successful choice should not be a compromise, but should satisfy both your visual aspirations and functional needs.

The location and nature of the existing structural floor will determine your available options. If you have a dry concrete ground floor, you are free to choose materials from the heaviest stone to carpet, or even paint. However, concrete is cold, as are stone or ceramic materials, and in rooms like kitchens, where you will be on your feet for long periods, you may want something warmer. In a bedroom you are likely to be looking for softness, so you might well go for carpet, cushioned vinyl or wood with rugs. If your existing floors are made of timber, they will be constructed of floor beams (or joists) overlaid with wooden boards or composite sheet. You may sand or paint these, or cover them with a thin overlay floor or carpet. It is possible to lay stone or thick tiles on wood, but you must make sure that the structure is strong enough to carry the weight.

On ground floors it is essential that your floor structure is fully damp-proofed – a damp floor can ruin expensive flooring materials and lead to other structural deterioration. If you are in doubt you should not lay any new floor finish until this has been verified and put right by a competent builder.

Bathrooms and kitchens place some of the most stringent demands on flooring, which needs to combine comfort with impermeability, as well as coping with bare feet or grease spills. Some materials can be ruled out from the beginning. Softwood, for example, will soon deteriorate and is best avoided. But you may have greater design flexibility than you imagine. For example, in a large kitchen only the area near the sink needs to be impervious to water; it could be laid with a narrow strip of tiles, while other areas could be timber, or carpet.

OPPOSITE *The limestone slabs in this entrance area reflect the light falling through the glass roof and serve to emphasize the inside/outside quality of the space.*

ABOVE *These old wide pine boards have been left unimproved and display the splits, edge damage and nail fixings accrued over time which all add to their character, as does their long unbroken length. Although they are dark, the glossiness reflects a lot of light into the room.*

ABOVE *Hallways make some of the greatest demands of a floor. The traditional character of this interior is emphasized by a hardwearing edged coir runner, which absorbs sound but still leaves visible a good proportion of the handsome boards.*

OPPOSITE *This stair is as much sculpture as anything else, the honey-coloured marble seeming to flow down the slot between the walls. Lights set into the treads make no difference to the sculptural quality of the surface, but the enhanced visibility they provide considerably improves the safety.*

Warmth & Sound

The temperature of a floor depends on the insulating property of the material and the extent to which it conducts heat. Good natural insulants, like cork or wool, are warm and retain the foot's natural heat, while stone, ceramic or mosaic draw the heat away. Timber is also warm, but if it consists only of a thin overlay it will, like other thin sheet materials, depend for its warmth on its underlying base – being colder when laid on concrete than on wood. Temperature is also affected by the orientation of the room. Floors can act as heat stores. When exposed to long hours of sunshine through a south-facing window they collect heat during the day and remain warm into the night. Dark solid floors   stone, tiles or mosaic – greatly assist this process, while carpeting inhibits it.

There are two different types of sound to consider when planning your floors: internal reverberation and the transmission of noise to rooms below. Sound bounces off hard flat surfaces, but is absorbed by soft finishes, so a hard floor in a sparsely furnished room will produce an echoing space. This can be counteracted with soft furnishings or by laying rugs on the floor. If you are keen to have minimal or hard furnishings but still wish to avoid an echoey feel, consider fitted carpet. Transmitted noise is harder to deal with. In bedrooms, which do not tend to generate much noise, carpet is the obvious answer. But where active areas, such as kitchens, playrooms or bathrooms, may cause disturbance to rooms beneath them and you do not want carpet, you could consider semi-soft surfaces like cork or, better still, cushioned vinyl. Noise is of particular concern in flats, and leasehold clauses often insist on carpet. If so, and you are determined to have a hard finish such as tiles, you may be allowed to lay these on a 'floating floor', where there is an absorbent layer separating the surface finish from the structural floor (see pages 173–4).

Durability & Traffic

Durability is a matter not only of wear, but of susceptibility to damage and loss of appearance over time. Some floors, such as stone, look just as good when worn, while carpet eventually becomes shabby. The long-term appearance of a material like wood will often depend on the quality of the applied finish and the care with which you maintain it. Your choice of floor should also take into account any medium- or long-term plans you may have. For example, if you want soft floor coverings but think you may want to undertake building work or move in the near future, you might consider buying rugs that you can remove and take with you, and laying them on a simple painted floor.

Use is normally defined as heavy, medium or light, and manufacturers grade their materials accordingly. For the heaviest use they apply the term 'contract'. Areas of heavy use will include circulation spaces and stairs, kitchens and utility areas. Medium use covers general living areas and family bathrooms; light use, bedrooms and en suite bathrooms. Most materials used for flooring will be suitable for all areas in the home, providing they are given the appropriate finish and protection. Carpet, however, is specifically graded into heavy, medium and light grades.

Maintenance & Cleaning

Certain areas of the home will be particularly prone to dirt: entrance halls, lobbies, utility rooms, garden rooms. Here you might adopt one of two approaches. You could either select a type of flooring which does not show the dirt, or accept the necessity for regular cleaning. Remember, too, that in your living-room flooring near garden doors – even if opened only occasionally – will need careful attention, and may dictate your overall strategy. For example rugs can be rolled up when children may be running through, while fitted carpet may need protection with overlay druggets. Ideally, try to develop a household habit of leaving outdoor shoes at the door, which will protect flooring and will make cleaning considerably easier.

If you can afford constant cleaning you are free to ignore the maintenance implications and choose whatever colours and finish you most prefer, such as whites and creams throughout the house. But in normal circumstances you should consider how often you are likely to be able to clean the floor, and how well. Be realistic. No floor, however beautiful, will be enjoyable if you are nightly obliged to get down on your hands and knees to scrub off the marks of muddy trainers! Many durable protecting sealers and polishes make it possible to have a sensible once or twice weekly cleaning programme on most floors. But it is the deep penetrating dirt or stains that need consideration, particularly in kitchen areas.

Safety

Floor surfaces are a crucial factor in preventing falls and need very careful consideration in relation to anticipated users and patterns of use and behaviour. There is no such thing as a non-slip floor: most products claim only to be 'slip resistant'. Generally speaking, the obvious rule applies: the smoother or more polished a surface the more slippery it will be, while rougher surfaces produce greater friction and hence greater resistance to slipping. However, once a foot is separated from the surface by a layer of liquid or grease, no flooring will prevent slipping. The best approach to safety is to make the surface rough enough to ensure that some part of it protrudes above any liquid film likely to be spilled on it and thus remains in contact with the foot. An extreme example of this is the kind of deeply studded tiles installed where there is a lot of water around swimming pools.

Changes of level or uneven surfaces are also dangerous, especially for visitors who are not familiar with the space. We very seldom look where we tread because we naturally assume the surface ahead is the same as the one we have just crossed – hence the danger of an unsuspected thick rug, particularly if it does not lie flat. Uneven steps are dangerous and will arise if you lay an additional surface on the floors at the top or bottom of an existing flight of steps.

Make sure that any unevenness and particularly any changes of level are made visually prominent, by altering the finish or colour of the floor and by providing good lighting. Illumination is particularly important for the elderly, who are likely to be unsure of both sight and step.

PATTERN DESIGN & COLOUR

Just as you need to determine practical requirements for your floor, so you should consider its appearance as part of your whole decorating scheme. You may want your room to be bright, up-beat and busy or soft, intimate and calm. You may prefer a crisp and ordered appearance or a rich, eclectic clutter. The options are endless, but it is important at the outset to develop a clear design concept which takes into account both your personal taste and the nature of the room itself. You may decide, for example, to try to mitigate the feeling of narrowness in a long room, or to impose a sense of formality in an asymmetric space, or to make a big draughty room feel more cosy. And you may have plans for a furniture arrangement which the flooring needs to enhance.

Our responses to the shapes, colours and patterns we see are determined by definite rules, and an understanding of these rules will enable you to formulate your design strategy and then to translate it into reality. The main visual ingredients at your disposal are pattern and line; the direction and size of the various elements in the floor; and the surface texture, light and colour. The skill lies in combining these different elements so that the eye reads them on the floor in ways that will create the feelings and responses to which you aspire.

Because the eye is attracted by areas of visual density or towards breaks in our overall visual field, it is possible to draw attention in particular directions by using pattern and line in a variety of ways on the floor. To make a passageway seem shorter, for example, you can lay bandings of colour across it, make diagonal joins in a plain material or combine contrasting colours. Longitudinal stripes and borders, on the other hand, increase the sense of perspective and lengthen a space. In small rooms you can lead the eye to the edges with borders, whereas in larger spaces a central pattern will provide a focal point.

In areas of circulation, such as hallways and open-plan living rooms, you can lead the eye from one point to another. The English architect Edwin Lutyens and the American architect Frank Lloyd Wright, for example, were extremely skilful at manipulating visual perception in this way, marking changes of direction with large circular slabs of stone, radial tiles or circular carpet designs.

This exceptional fourteenth-century floor in the Popes Palace at Avignon could provide inspiration for modern designers. The limited *palette of earthy tones and the simple decorative motifs on the tiles are given depth by a thick clear lead overglaze.*

11

Simple regular shapes of squares and rectangles form the essential building blocks of most patterns. These diagrams demonstrate how variety can be achieved using these basic elements. On this page units of the same size have been simply laid in regular, diagonal or staggered lines. The diagrams opposite show just a few of the more complex patterns that can be produced by using different sizes of one basic shape, such as a square, by combining rectangles and squares, by changing the direction in which the units are laid, or by taking two shapes and varying the colour, as in the tumbling blocks pattern. Although the individual forms are simple, the permutations are almost endless and each has its own very different visual effect. Add to this variety of pattern elements of texture as well as colour, and the design opportunities are infinite. Similar variation and building of designs from a few simple units can be achieved with other combinations of shapes, such as hexagons with triangles or octagons with squares.

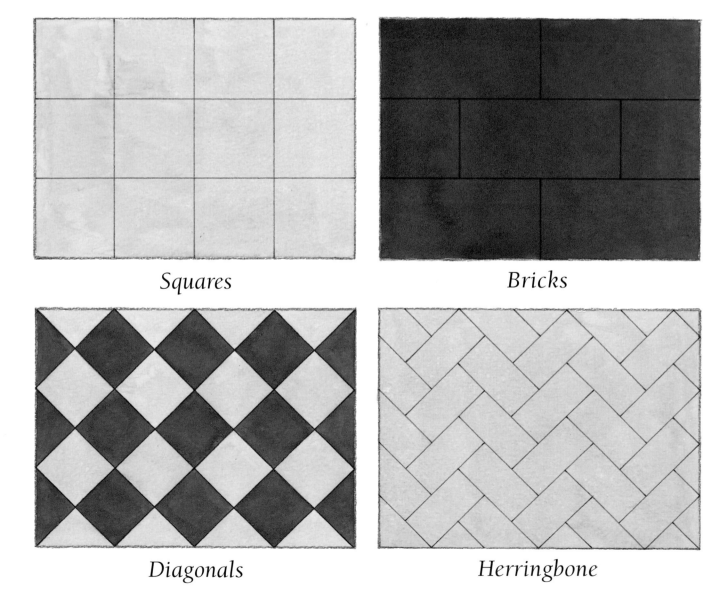

Squares

Bricks

Diagonals

Herringbone

Squares & rectangles

Key squares

Reversed axis

Basketweave

Small & large squares

Tumbling blocks

OPPOSITE *The bold blue and white design – a large Greek key pattern – is complemented by the subtle variety of colour and veining in the stones, creating an unmistakeable feeling of cool.*

ABOVE *This pattern of diagonal lines breaks up the floor into large areas of dark and light tone, reducing the apparent length of this long corridor. Joints have been scored into the surface to crisply define the areas of colour and suggest the meeting points of stone blocks. This floor demonstrates the timelessness of bold geometrical patterns in a traditional setting.*

Our in-built sense of balance and our consciousness of horizontal and vertical mean that the same flooring pattern will take on different qualities according to its relationship with the walls. The simplest example of this can be seen in square slabs or tiles: when laid on the diagonal they produce a much greater sense of vitality and movement than when the squares run at right-angles to the lines of the walls. Similarly, we can suggest formality or informality by using symmetrical or asymmetrical shapes. Wavy, radiating and, in particular, Catherine wheel patterns all create an impression of movement and dynamism. The larger the asymmetrical elements the greater will be their dynamic effect. Particularly powerful patterns are created where an asymmetrical pattern is overlaid onto a regular balanced pattern or grid, thereby creating a contrast.

To lend a specific feel to a room you might also consider using patterns or motifs based on recognizable objects. Elaborate floral patterns create a lush, organic atmosphere, while simplified flower motifs or even figures provide an impression of lively freshness. The use of stylized animals or everyday objects suggests the naive innocence associated with folk art.

When choosing patterned floors you should bear in mind that our brains take considerable amounts of information 'as read', so any motif used repetitively will tend to be absorbed into an overall visual texture and assumed to be regular – unless something causes the eye to register otherwise. This aspect of the way the brain functions explains why certain patterns appear to be three-dimensional. In a traditional basketweave pattern, for example, a simple arrangement of interlocking rectangles, some complete and others interrupted, implies that the interrupted blocks continue behind the complete ones. Our brains fill in the missing information. Conversely, a single motif used in only a few instances will either gain in emphasis or may prove distracting. It is important, therefore, to achieve the correct balance between repetition and strong individual accents, so that the pattern becomes neither boring nor disturbing.

As you develop your design, combining colour and shapes, remember that your floor will be viewed not statically, but as you move over it, and the effect of this movement must be taken into account. Some parts of a pattern will be seen at a distance and thus from a low angle, while those parts directly beneath your feet are seen almost flat on. This variation in the angle reduces the apparent size of pattern in larger spaces so components such as tiles appear to recede into the distance, an effect that can be exploited to alter the perception of a space.

Colour

The colour of your floor is among the most important factors in creating the feel of a room. Responses to colour are bound to be subjective, but there are generally agreed properties assigned to specific colours which are particularly relevant to a choice of floor. These are connected to ideas of visual excitement and repose, of hot or cold, and of distance or dimension.

The colour which creates the most repose in the eye is mid-grey, which can be obtained by mixing any two complementary colours opposite each other on the colour wheel (shown overleaf) – either green and red, or yellow and violet, or orange and blue. Conversely, the primary colours in their undiluted form will

ABOVE *The basic colour wheel.*

BELOW *By limiting the colour palette but randomizing the layout a modern effect can be achieved.* FAR BELOW *A quieter but still interesting effect can be made by limiting the design to different tones of the same colour.*

create the very opposite effect of repose. This is why grey is often chosen when neutral undemonstrative floors are needed in working environments; indeed the word grey is a euphemism for a lack of excitement. This may be a quality you wish to exploit; and if you are aiming for an unostentatious, calm floor, greys or beiges may be appropriate. But remember that there are shades of the same colour which vary from cool to warm – and particularly among the greys.

Combinations of colour can be used to create excitement and interest, without necessarily clashing or jarring. This can be true even when the shades in question are bright and powerful, providing that they are complementary. Where colour contrasts are most intense, the effect tends to be vigorous, optimistic, bright and eye-catching, as is demonstrated by the bright gay colours invariably present in folk art. The 'prettiness' or folksiness associated with elements of bright colour or design can be used to valuable effect to enliven gloomy or dull interiors.

Possibly the most frequent basis for the way we choose colour is the characteristic that can best be described as 'temperature'. Experiments have shown that people can perceive a temperature difference of as much as seven degrees between so-called hot and cold colours, regardless of the real room temperature, and that hot colours generate feelings of excitement while cooler ones induce a sense of repose. Roughly speaking, colours fall into the following temperature range: at the hottest end are yellow, yellow-orange, orange, orange-red, red and red-violet, while yellow-green, green, blue-green, blue-violet and violet are cool. But again, you should remember that intermediate shades can appear warmer or colder, depending on the colours from which they are mixed.

Colours can express many other feelings and contrasts: shady or sunny, earthy or airy, far or near. Bluer tones appear to recede, while reds appear to advance, and these effects can be exploited to create a sense of distance in a floor design. Any two colours separated by black will seem sharper, brighter and luminous than those separated by white – a point you may wish to bear in mind when choosing colours for borders or joints, or when making tartan patterns. Our perception of pattern in general will be affected by colour. A restless pattern can be calmed by use of colours which are closely related, while a balanced design can be rendered dynamic by contrasting colours. Colour is linked also with a sense of atmosphere: the earthy reds and browns of terracotta, or blue-grey slate, will create a sensibly homely and informal feel for a kitchen, while pale marble or limestone will suggest a greater formality in a dining room.

In many cases, the selection of colour will be determined not only by your design concept and the nature and qualities of the space, but also by the material which best meets the functional demands of the room. In a country kitchen you may wish to use a local stone which only comes in one colour, whereas in a city apartment, where a soft floor is necessary for acoustic reasons, you have the freedom of choice afforded by carpet. If you decide to go for natural materials, such as grasses, rush or coir, colour and texture become inseparable.

OPPOSITE *Here the designer has broken away from conventional thinking to produce a floor so striking that it defies categorization. The cool glazed tiles are used as free compositional elements on a flat ground of warm pink tiles. The eye-catching pattern expands the space by linking it through the two doorways.*

Scale

When thinking about which materials you want for your floor, you should consider the relation between the size of individual elements and the dimensions of the whole space, since this can have a marked effect on the feel of a room. A large hallway, for example, will appear grand and imposing if floored with big slabs of stone, but less monumental and more domestic if laid with smaller elements like encaustic tiles. This is something to remember when choosing materials in a showroom or from a small sample. Wherever possible, try to obtain a few pieces of the materials and assess their size within the context of the room, as you would do their colour. These considerations apply equally to pattern. The effect produced by differently sized elements within a space arises in part from the ability of the eye to resolve definition. In a large room, where you are at a distance from some areas of the floor, fine patterns or repeats will not be read distinctly and will appear as a uniform surface. To be legible as individual motifs they need to be bigger. On the other hand, in a small room, more diminutive motifs or patterns will be clearly legible.

Borders

Defined borders in your flooring can draw the eye to different parts of a room and create emphasis in specific areas. You may wish, for example, to disguise the fact that a room is slightly asymmetric with the use of a symmetrical edging, or to focus attention on the centre of the space by surrounding a central field with a contrasting border. Remember, however, that thick or multiple concentric borders will tend to reduce the apparent size of a room.

Any frame lends importance to the area within it, providing there is sufficient difference between the two. A busy border around an equally busy field merely confuses the eye and brain. A strong, rich frame around a plain field makes the centre appear more significant, imparting a confident and assured feel to the room. A calm floor with subtle interest can be created when tiles or stones are laid at right-angles to the walls in a central field, surrounded by a border of the same materials but laid diagonally.

Borders also allow you to introduce elements of colour and pattern which would not be suitable as part of an overall design. For example, in a floor of rectangular plain tiles, the border might contain Greek key patterns or more curvilinear motifs, such as scrolls or flowers. The graphic quality of script can be used effectively, as it was in traditional Islamic art, to make borders which include text or dates.

LEFT *These two floors of similar black and white squares demonstrate the effect of different sized pieces, the smaller ones creating a greater sense of perspective because they appear to recede so much more than the larger ones.*

OPPOSITE *The strongly delineated border along the edge of this parquet floor helps give coherence to a space containing a variety of uncoordinated wall elements.*

Texture & Warmth

The textural qualities of floors appeal to eye and touch and may have a radical effect on how we perceive both the floor and the room as a whole. Because we register and focus on incidents, perfectly straight and even manufactured products provide less visual interest than the irregular colouring and texture of natural materials. This is probably why weather-worn surfaces, with their lumps and bumps, often appear so much more attractive than newly built ones, and why the slight irregularities in the edges of hand-cut stone, hand-riven slates or hand-made tiles make them more appealing than machine-cut materials.

Tactile sensations are very important in a floor, because feet are sensitive to surface changes. Sink into thick pile carpet and you will experience a sense of luxury and even of physical warmth. Scrape along rough cobbles, on the other hand, and you will be aware of a rugged tough quality; while smooth polished marble or glazed tiles suggest clean order or sophistication.

Our experience of warmth and cold in different materials is not simply a matter of touch. The awareness of what something feels like also influences our visual perceptions of it. We say that stone, mosaic or glass are cold-looking, not because we can actually see the cold, but because we have learned by touch that they are so. When considering your choice of floor, you need to be conscious of the messages imparted by different materials. Mosaic in particular is perceived as cool not only because it is cold to the touch but because of its associations with certain types of stone interiors and its shimmering water-like appearance. The more polished the material, the cooler it tends to look – polished slate or granite seem less warm than when riven, glazed tiles cooler than rough.

Light

As the largest surface in the room, the floor plays a crucial part in reflecting the light that enters the space and will affect its overall colour and atmosphere. In the northern hemisphere, north light is the most even and unchanging, and appears colder than light from a southern sky, while the opposite is true south of the equator. So in a room facing away from the midday sun you should be wary of materials like blue slate that look cold, and consider instead the warmer tones of terracotta, wood or cork. If you wish to lighten a room, the reflectivity of the floor is crucial: select pale colours – light limestones, white or cream marble, pale ceramics or carpets, light woods. However, if the floor is too light and reflects dazzling sunlight, it will be uncomfortable. Rooms with a sunny aspect or conservatories which get hot in summer might benefit from floors of blues, greens or greys.

Light will also influence our perception of texture. Low sidelight emphasizes any differences in the surface, while light directly overhead or sunless light minimizes them. This is why painters traditionally favoured studios which were not exposed to sunlight, where deep harsh shadows could be avoided. When deciding the degree of textured finish, you should therefore consider the position and size of windows. In west- or east-facing rooms, where the sunlight enters at a lower angle, deep textures are less necessary.

OPPOSITE *The plain austerity of this room is given an almost palatial sense of warmth and luxury by the contrast between the boards and the soft antique rugs, a kelim in the foreground and a knotted pile rug behind it.*

ABOVE *In this classic room with wooden casing and mahogany-coloured fittings, an obvious timber floor would have been dark and traditional, yet here the designer has painted the boards a pale colour to reflect light and brighten the whole space.*

Appropriateness

Having taken all the practical and aesthetic considerations into account, you will also need to address the complex question of what messages your selected floor material will convey. Is it appropriate to the type of building and that part of your home in which you will be using it? Does it accord with the physical and cultural context of your home and with your own life-style? If it does, the floor will feel natural and 'right' for you, your family and friends. If it does not, the floor may well always feel uncomfortable, regardless of how wonderful the material itself may be.

Today you can as easily use Italian marble in America or French terracotta in England as you can the stone from the quarry nearby; but while this plethora of available materials offers you great opportunity, it also represents a potential pitfall. Flooring showrooms and catalogues can be dangerously seductive with their array of materials and colours from all over the world. When considering a material it is best to start by looking carefully at examples of the best interiors of their period to see how the flooring materials work with the architecture and all aspects of the setting. The floors that stand the test of time – whether modern or ancient – are chosen so that they are appropriate to all aspects of their context. Tempting as it may be to try something exotic or unusual, you need to think about its suitability for the setting. For a country cottage, flagstones in the kitchen and honest boards from local sources in the bedrooms will be far more fitting than foreign marble or exotic hardwoods. By contrast, however, an apartment in a sophisticated city block reached by an elegant lift can accommodate more unusual materials, while rustically natural flooring will feel over-crude and out of place.

Materials carry strong associations with the places from which they come and these messages are most important to consider when selecting a floor. It feels no more right to encounter Welsh mountain slates in Italy than it does Provençal terracotta farmhouse tiles in a New York apartment. A white sea pebble floor at the coast is entirely appropriate, while it would seem perverse and ostentatious in a mountainous region full of slate and far from the sea. Exceptionally an 'anything goes' approach can work, but as a general rule the use of materials inappropriate to their context can be as unsettling as someone arriving at a formal banquet in beach wear.

Outlandish, surprising and inappropriate floors might be exciting and fun to enliven hallways or bathrooms, but in living rooms they are unlikely to prove satisfying and comfortable in the long run. However fanciful your imagination or extensive your funds may be, there is no merit in bold, powerful and exquisitely complicated floors for their own sake. Not only will a plain floor provide a restful environment, it will also allow you the flexibility to change the other elements in the room, which you are likely to alter more often than the floor.

Using local materials with a comfortable sense of authenticity does not necessarily mean that you should aim for slavish historical correctness. As your floor will be read as a part of the building fabric, you should take your cue from its architectural style. You do not need to copy it, but there should be sensitive interplay between the floor and the building's architecture, as well as all the elements of the space within which your floor is laid.

ABOVE AND OPPOSITE *Two contrasting spaces demonstrate the importance of appropriate flooring. In the formal interior opposite carefully chiselled and symmetrically laid diagonal stone tiles match the symmetry of the furniture. The large flagstones in the informal cottage interior above are newly laid but convey an unsophisticated country feel in keeping with the thick masonry walls and shelf.*

Creating Calm & Repose

We are so bombarded with visual messages and stimuli in our daily lives that when it comes to creating an enjoyable home I believe it is important to err towards calm and reposeful interiors. The floor has a major part to play in this. You may have good reason to want a powerful, busy effect, but in this event I would suggest that it be confined to one or two locations. Since your floor forms the visual background to your decoration and furniture, try to keep it simple.

Qualities of calm and repose are mainly a function of eye movement. Our eyes can only focus on a small area at a time, and if called upon to take in more than this, they will continually be pulled in different directions. This is why fussiness of line and pattern or visual clutter (unless achieved with such skill as to be in careful balance) create a sense of restlessness. The universal appeal of Japanese or American Shaker houses with their plain tatami mats or timber board floors, of simple modern interiors or plain white Mediterranean architecture with tiled floors is proof of how the absence of strong visual accents in the floor contributes to peaceful and timelessly satisfying rooms.

Strong contrasts, whether of colour, line or shape, are disruptive and keep our brains in a state of constant visual activity. Compare, for example, the effect on the eye of a crazy-paving floor with that of simple, equal squares. Irregularity and fussy contrast produce what can best be described as 'visual noise', while symmetry and balance play a major part in those classical designs which are universally appreciated for their harmony.

Yet although repetition of simple components can create calm, it can also become tedious, especially over larger areas. To introduce diversity to a regular pattern, you can buy hand-made carpets or tiles which have subtle differences in colour, texture or motif. In a stone or tiled floor, small cabochons or key squares will produce a similar effect of variety within a tranquil framework.

To maintain a sense of repose when using patterns and motifs, you should decide from the outset where the weight of visual accent is to fall: on a foreground motif or on a background. When the two are equal, attention flickers continuously from one to the other, causing unease and restlessness. It is also important to consider where and how to make joints in materials. Unless you want the joint to attract the eye or to be seen as part of a pattern, it should be as discreet and as tight as possible, particularly in materials such as slate, stone, tiles or timber. It is a very common fault today, arising from the decline in craftsmanship, that joints tend to be overlarge. Look at the simplest Victorian ceramic floor and you will see how tightly the pieces butt together.

Simplicity is a powerful design statement in itself and conveys confidence, assuredness and certainty. Plain good-quality materials, well but simply laid, can give lasting satisfaction.

In this converted London bank building, the linoleum squares are of a size appropriate to the scale of the space. The absence of borders allows the pattern to run through adjacent doorways, and the quiet colours help to create an assured simplicity.

STONE

Mountains and river beds provide stones from the modest to the majestic, giving to stone buildings a strong natural and local character. Moving stone over long distances was once the prerogative of the wealthy, but modern transport has made stones from around the world widely available. Wherever it is used, stone creates a sense of solidity that will last well beyond the life of those who lay it. The feeling of rock and stone underfoot is one of strength and permanence.

The earliest houses had beaten-earth floors, but as building techniques grew more sophisticated these were superseded by local stone cut into square 'flags' or by stone pebbles. Aristocratic Roman homes had floors of travertine or marble. In England, mud floors continued even in grand domestic buildings during the early Middle Ages, although there are a few examples of chalk floors and of pebbles and gravel mixed with mud. By the late medieval and Renaissance periods, however, important houses were being floored with a variety of stones, including slate, sandstone and limestone while granite cobbles were seen in rural buildings.

Elsewhere in Europe, multicoloured stones were arranged to create floors with complex geometric designs in churches and public buildings, and from the sixteenth century patterned marble floors appeared even in relatively modest domestic interiors. Seventeenth-century English architects were influenced by such styles, and the splendid Baroque floors of Castle Howard in Yorkshire and Chatsworth in Derbyshire reflected the European interest in illusion and trompe l'oeil. In North America, the European tradition was copied only in a few of the grander houses of the colonial period. A fine example can be seen in the eighteenth-century Drayton Hall, South Carolina, where Portland limestone and Welsh red sandstone were used to form a classic chequerboard design.

For the most part historical floors, whether plain or patterned, were made of dressed stone, but more recently there has been renewed interest in rough textures. The early twentieth-century architects Frank Lloyd Wright and Marcel Breuer combined randomly shaped undressed slabs with wood and flat plastered surfaces in their interiors, the muscularity of the natural stone emphasized by contrast with the smoothness around it. Their designs show that it is not necessary to emulate styles of the past when using traditional materials.

Stones are classified in three categories according to their geological formation: sedimentary – the sandstones and limestones; metamorphic – slates, marbles and quartzes; and igneous – granite. Each type has distinctive characteristics and imparts particular qualities to the space in which it is used.

The floor in this eighteenth-century Parisian hallway is both sophisticated and simple, with its classical pattern of white and black. The plain border contains the space and accommodates the stone steps on the left and the doorway to the right. The roughness of the reclaimed black and white marble lends an appropriate feeling of age, while uncomplicated furnishing allows the floor to be appreciated in all its beauty.

BELOW *This 'gallery' in a traditional Cotswold stone house derives its timeless quality from the simple grandeur of its large York stone flags complemented by the chunky timber of the roof and windows. Underfloor heating leaves the walls free of radiators.*

Limestone & Sandstone

Limestone and sandstone are both sedimentary stones, formed by the accumulation and compression of mud, clay, ashes, fossils and other debris. This accumulation gives sand- and limestones their characteristic horizontal bedding planes. These planes lack horizontal adhesion, which is why some older stones, in particular sandstones such as York stone, have layers, some of which have flaked away. This degradation, however, is due primarily to the effect of weathering over many years – layering is seldom seen in newly quarried stone and is hardly likely to occur where the stone is laid indoors. As both sand- and limestone have very similar characteristics in appearance, performance and use, they are treated here as a single group.

In sandstone, the sediments contain silica, which gives the stone its somewhat rough, friable texture and occasional glitter. However, it is the presence of other compounds, including haematite and clay minerals, in addition to the silica, which is responsible for the very wide variety of colours in which sandstone can be found, ranging from yellowish white to various shades of buff, golden brown, beige and red, as well as blue grey.

There are three types of limestones, only two of which are suitable for floors. Oolitic limestone is composed of concentric layers of calcite that have gathered around the fragments of shell and fossils which give the stone its characteristic appearance – Portland stone in particular has a high proportion of such fragments. Crystalline limestone is formed as underground water evaporates and crystallizes from the sedimentary bed – the best-known example is travertine. Organic limestone, such as chalk, is an accumulation of vegetable and animal matter and is generally too soft for floors.

The natural holes and pitting in the stones – particularly marked in travertine and Portland stone – occur when soft matter is washed out of the surface or air pockets remain during formation. When such stones are used externally, either for paving or walling, these pockets are normally left, but for internal use they need to be filled. Although they vary in hardness, most limestones on the market will be suitable for floors, except those you can dent or rub with your nails. The choice is simply one of colour and texture. The stone comes in a wide range of colours, from creamy whites, plain and flecked beiges, pale ochre yellows, pale greys and grey-greens to nearly black. Although most stone cut today is selected and batched for its uniformity, it is possible to find a variety of shades within one kind of stone, particularly among older flags. Even in a single slab there may be a surprising richness of different tones.

To form slabs and tiles, the stone is not split but sawn, and texture is given to the face by the saw, chisel or polisher. Sand- and limestones are available in honed or sanded finishes. The honed finish, although even and quite silky smooth, is very matt, which gives a surface glow more subtle than that of the highly polished stones and emphasizes the lovely natural sediment formations and fossils in the material. A rough sawn finish, while initially rougher than honed, will smooth down with use. The sanded finish is not silky smooth but has a very slight roughness to the touch. This makes it particularly suitable for use in wet areas of the house.

Sand- and limestone can be bought in a range of standard tile sizes, normally

BELOW *The pale smoothness of limestone (top) contrasts with the rich rustic-looking terracotta of a textured York stone (bottom).*

40cm (15¾in) square or 40×60cm (15¾×23½in), and in random running lengths usually between about 30 and 50cm (11¾ and 19¾in) wide, all at a thickness of 20mm (¾in). Larger slabs are available up to 1×1m (39½×39½in) and 30mm (1¼in) thick. European quarry suppliers are flexible and deliver quickly, and it is therefore easy to order stone in any shape or size. As the slabs are cut at the quarry, it should not necessarily be more expensive to do this – however, some suppliers add a premium for non-standard sizes. In an appropriate context, older properties can look very good with floors of reclaimed flags of sandstone or limestone, such as York stone. Often these come from city footpaths that are being renewed, or from farmhouses or cellars, and they are worn and uneven, as well as being thick – sometimes up to 10 to 12.5cm (4 or 5in).

Stone tiles, whether old or new, can be laid by either the thick-bed or the thin-bed method, as discussed on page 176. It is always best to keep the joints as tight as possible, preferably not wider than 3mm (⅛in) for new tiles; for old slabs the joints will vary according to the quality of the edges. To prevent staining, it is advisable to apply a first coat of sealer before grouting. On old slabs ensure that the joint does not cover attractive worn edges but sits slightly recessed, so that the stone remains the dominant visual material. It is possible to use one of the proprietary grouts, a mix of sand and lime with a small amount of cement, or simply sand and cement. Some suppliers will provide a grout mix to match the stone. If this is not obtainable, choose a proprietary coloured grout or on darker stones darken the joints with black boot polish to make them recede. If the stone contains natural crevices which would be impractical on interior floors, some installers will fill the surface by dragging grout across the stone and then wiping it off to leave a residue in the crevices. Otherwise, grout must not be dragged across the surface of the stone, as it is not easy to remove.

Any cement or adhesive left on the tiles during installation should be taken off immediately before it hardens. For cement film you can use grade 3 or 4 steel wool. Removing hardened cement from used stones is particularly difficult. It will need to be taken off with cement remover or even chipped or ground off. Although these techniques are likely to damage the stone, in my view an old flag with some surface damage looks considerably better than one left covered with cement. Abrasion marks can be smoothed with wire wool.

Although durable, these stones are porous and need to be sealed against dirt and stains. If limestone is left untreated, the surface will 'break open' and over the course of a year or two it will develop a self-protecting 'skin' through oxidation. However, it is before this skin develops that the natural pore-like holes in the surface will catch grit and dirt, and the floor will absorb stains. It is therefore essential to seal the surface as soon as it is laid. The best method of sealing is by silicone impregnation, as it scarcely changes the colour or the surface texture but allows the floor to age naturally, providing it is regularly swept and washed with a neutral soap. This natural ageing does not occur when the floor is sealed with one of the resin-based sealants, which simply put a surface skin on the stone. These tend to be used in areas where little maintenance will be provided, but they are too slippery for wet areas and are prone to bubbling if moisture gets underneath them. One of the most attractive characteristics of lime- and sandstones is that they mellow and improve with age and, if well maintained, will retain a subtle glow.

OPPOSITE *These rough old limestone flags are entirely in keeping with the rugged walls and beams of this French house, and are of a size appropriate to the small scale of the room. The direction of the slabs draws the eye into the bed recess. The pinkish tones of the stone are picked up in the red upholstery, while the ornateness of the furnishing is heightened by the contrasting roughness of wall and floor surfaces.*

New, smooth, machine-cut slabs of limestone laid in a regular grid create an opulent but unostentatious floor for this calm interior, allowing the powerful curved forms of the dark wood-framed furniture to read clearly. The pale glow of the stone reflects the maximum amount of light pouring in from the window, so that the whole room appears clear and airy.

In this Sardinian house, the refreshing combination of bright ceramic-tiled stairs and a floor made from different coloured limestones with a stone balustrade and arches creates an interior *which is both relaxing and imposing. What at first appears to be randomly scattered multicoloured stone on the floor is, in fact, a subtle geometric pattern of squares and rectangles.*

Slate

The word slate derives from the French *esclater* 'to split', and a material is generally classed as a slate if it splits along natural planes of cleavage to form thin slabs or tiles. Slate is a metamorphic rock formed some 350–500 million years ago when clays and rocks were subject to the intense natural compression underground which produced its characteristic linear planes. This formation under immense pressure makes slate extremely dense and almost as durable as marble and granite when used on floors. It is inert, resistant to frost and chemicals, absorbs only oil or oily compounds and, unless gouged with sharp points, its finish and appearance will hardly change over time.

Slate is found in the oldest mountainous regions of the world. Each quarry produces a slate with a unique colour, composition and durability. Those from European sources have a traditional colour palette ranging from near black, greys and blues, through blue-purples and grey-greens. Slates of a wholly different range of colours are now available from Africa, Brazil and China. Many of these are much softer, but most are still suitable for flooring. They have an extraordinary variety of rich autumn colours, from browny golds, rusts and oranges to pale pinks and even creams, as well as some similar to the European hues. Each slate has a marked and irregular colour variation, revealing its composition from flowing sedimentary muds. On a floor these coloured slates are best used sparingly. Although a few sample tiles can look sumptuous, a large area can be overpowering. The less variegated slates, in contrast, form a quiet background.

Slate is ideal for carving and takes different textures well, which permits the creation of patterns of different textured finishes within the same type of slate. It is possible, for example, to have roughly textured borders surrounding polished areas of the same slate, creating a rich but subtle interest in the floor.

New slate normally comes in one of five finishes: 'riven' (hand-split to uneven thickness); 'flame-textured' (machine-cut to even thickness), in which the surface is literally flaked off by flame and left rough; 'sanded', which is flat but not polished, with a slightly abrasive finish; 'honed', which is smooth and silky but matt; and polished, which is the smoothest and shiniest, although the extent of shine varies with the make-up of different slates, some of which cannot be polished to glass-like smoothness. A riven finish provides good slip resistance in most situations. Being generally softer and flakier, Chinese, African and Brazilian slates can be worked only to a fairly heavily textured finish.

Some of the most attractive slate floors are made from old hand-cut slate flags smoothed through long use and usually originating from old farmhouses or the work areas in large country properties. Occasionally they are found in sizes up to 120, 150 and even 180cm (4, 5 and 6ft) by 60 or 90cm (2 or 3ft), but normally they come in batches sorted into similar widths (usually 40 to 55cm (16 to 21in), with random lengths from 40 up to 75 or sometimes 100cm

FROM TOP *Umbria slate; African multi-coloured slate; Beijing green slate.*

OPPOSITE *Texture and contrast are paramount in this country interior where the roughness of white walls and old timbers contrasts with the large, roughly cut but sparklingly polished slate flags. The wide* cement infill between the flagstones and the wall and at the edge of the stairs are all part of this room's integrity. No further adornment is needed, apart from one or two pieces of equally bold furniture.

(16 up to 30 or 40in). They usually have an upper face that is even, but not absolutely flat, and can be 5–10cm (2–4in) thick. Slate flags must be laid in thick sand and cement screed, on a concrete base, with a screed depth of at least 38mm (1½in). It is best to buy old flags before you lay the concrete so you can be sure you have allowed sufficient depth for the floor. If you must lay the base before you find a source of slate, allow at least 15cm (6in) for the total floor thickness so as not to limit your choice. One of the beauties of old flags lies in their uneven hand-riven edges. Although most pieces can be laid uncut, inevitably some will need trimming, and it is important to discuss this with your layer. Cutting is easily done with a portable handgrinder, but you should distress the cut edge with a slate hammer to resemble the older hand-cut edges.

New slabs are machine-cut to an even thickness and have even edges, which can be distressed if required. Large slabs can be ordered in any size; the thickness will usually be about 20 to 30mm (¾ to 1¼in) depending upon the size. New flag floors look best when the traditional pattern of running lengths is used – that is a pattern in which slabs of random lengths but equal widths are laid in straight lines. This looks most attractive if the width varies in each row.

Slate tiles come in a wide variety of sizes, of which the most common are smaller squares of 20cm (7⅞in), 30cm (11¾in) and 40cm (15¾in), all 9 to 12mm (⅜ to ½in) thick, and larger ones of 50cm (19¾in) and 60cm (23½in), either 15 or 20mm (⅝ or ¾in) thick, or random length 'planks' 15, 20 or 30cm (around 6, 8 or 11¾in) wide and 20mm (¾in) thick. Tiles can be cut to order, and squares with corners cut for cabochon inserts and other patterns are easily obtained, allowing tiles to be laid in various designs.

The methods for laying slate are the same as those described for laying limestone (see page 176). Slate should be sealed to prevent the absorption of oily stains, and this is essential for the newer softer slates. Proprietary sealers are available, usually from the slate supplier. These are either water- or solvent-based, and both types have advantages and disadvantages. Water-based sealants look good for a while – apart from a slight darkening, they make little change to the finish – but they deteriorate with repeated washing. Solvent-based sealants are more durable, but they must be very carefully and thinly applied so as not to give the effect of thick varnish. To avoid ruining expensive stones, it is crucial that these finishes are applied strictly according to the instructions. Some specialists advise against the use of oil products, but I have sealed a floor with a mixture of three parts turpentine to one part linseed oil, rubbed well in, that looked very attractive and needed no renewal for many years, although this treatment is only suitable for softer slates.

To clean slate it is generally enough to dry buff with a nylon pad. Less frequently you can vacuum away loose dirt and scrub with a light pad or brush using neutral detergent in warm water. Rinse until the water is clear, then buff up when the slate is dry. Any substances which adhere stubbornly can be scraped away with a light abrasive pad. To remove oil and grease stains, use white spirit, for tea and coffee wash with neutral detergent solution.

This kitchen is functional but decorative, deriving its richness from the natural colours of the slate and the variegated grain in the wood of the units. The square pattern of the flags reflects the rigidity of line imposed on the whole room.

Marble

Like slate, marble is a metamorphic rock, formed by heat or pressure on limestone. However, unlike slate, marble has a very dense crystalline structure which gives it a special luminous quality when polished, and with appropriate tools it can be cut to the finest detail.

The variety of natural compounds contained in marble gives it its extraordinary range of colourings, and its heavy figuring is caused by the original bedding structure and the folding of the rock during formation. Marble is found in many mountainous regions, including those of North America, Mexico, North Africa and many European countries, particularly Italy, Portugal, Greece and Norway. The marble from each region has its own particular colour, and many marbles are named after their place of origin.

The extensive colour range and suitability for precision cutting make marble versatile for inlay and multicoloured work, whether for large bold patterns, plain areas with elaborate borders or isolated motifs. Because of the expense and the level of skill required, traditional hand-inlay work has been largely replaced today by a range of precut patterns available from specialists. Since decorative marble flooring will tend to dominate a room, particularly one of normal domestic size, perhaps the most suitable designs for such spaces are the traditional understated patterns of squares of pale marble with inset key squares of either slate or a darker marble.

Marble is excellent for use in wet areas. As it is impervious to water and hygienically smooth, it is particularly suitable for bathrooms – although it does have the disadvantage of being slippery when wet. But despite their denseness, most marbles are susceptible to staining and corrosion by acidic solutions, and they are therefore best avoided in kitchens, where granite is probably a more suitable choice.

Marble is available in a variety of finishes. The most common are polished, with a high gloss; eggshell, with a slight gloss and 'no. 3 honed' or 'no. 4 honed', which are matt. Because it is machined to very high tolerances, the joints can be kept to an absolute minimum. Stock tile sizes are generally 30×30cm (11¾×11¾in), 40×40cm (15¾×15¾in), 30×15cm (11¾×6in) or 40×20cm (15¾×8in), all between 7 and 10mm (¼ and ⅜in) thick. However, as with other stone products, larger suppliers can provide slabs to suit your design requirements. Bear in mind that large slabs can be difficult to lay because once set down on wet bedding the suction makes them hard to move. Like other stones, marble requires virtually no maintenance. Clean water applied with a chamois will remove all but the most stubborn dirt. Occasionally, a floor might need a wash with a sulphate-free soap.

OPPOSITE *Stephen Sills and James Huniford, the owners and designers of this guest cottage in New York, have created an unusual interior using marble cobbles rather than polished marble slab. The rough pale stone reflects light into the room and contrasts with the ornate furniture.*

RIGHT *Coloured marble makes a positive statement whether used on its own or in sophisticated pattern work. From top to bottom: Venetian marble verde; Venetian marble rosso; thin slivers of coloured and polished marble inset in a plain floor to create an ornate border.*

Granite

Granite is the only igneous rock generally used in interiors. It is distinguished by its crystalline formation, produced when the earth's molten crust cooled some 5,000 million years ago. Granites come from all parts of the world, the best-known sources being Spain, France, Portugal, Scandinavia, Brazil, Sri Lanka, India and South Africa. As the stones from different locations are formed from different compounds, each has its characteristic appearance, ranging in texture from large crystals to tiny granules and in colour from black to dark greys, pale greys, greys tinted with blue, blues, green-blacks, reds and pinks. Because they are so dense, granites are impervious to almost everything and extremely hard. As the most durable of all known building stones, they are very difficult to work, and because of dwindling resources they are very costly.

Granite is available in the same honed, polished or etched finishes as marble, but in the case of granite different finishes will create wholly different colours and characteristics. Polishing gives the granite a deeper, richer colour, as well as revealing the natural structure and the colour variations in the crystalline granules. The most common sizes of granite tiles for floors are squares of 30×30cm (11¾×11¾in) and 40×40cm (15¾×15¾in) and rectangles of 40×60cm (15¾×23½in), all usually 10mm (⅜in) thick, although tiles up to 20mm (¾in) thick are available and a wide variety of other sizes can be found. Granite should be laid with as narrow a joint as possible

If you would like the opulent effect of a stone floor for your kitchen, granite is a more appropriate choice than marble as it does not stain. But as polished granite floors are made very slippery by water or grease, it might be better to choose an etched surface in such areas, rather than a polished one. You could combine etched and polished surfaces in a larger kitchen/dining room, for example, by using a wide etched granite border in front of the kitchen units with a lighter contrasting marble for the dining area. Keep in mind that when seen close up a granite sample may have a rich variety of colours in the granules, but at a distance or over larger areas it will appear to have a uniform colour which makes it appear very different from the more obvious figuration and veining so obvious in some marbles.

The durability of granite means that it requires no sealer and that maintenance is extremely easy. Cleaning is the same as for marble. Etched and honed surfaces require only a scrub in clean water, possibly with a neutral cleaning solution. Avoid chemical cleaners or industrial solvents. Although granite floors can be supplied with a variety of finishes, like other stone floors they should never be coated with floor polish and buffed. The film built up on the surface of the stone by regular applications of polish accumulates more dirt than the unpolished stone.

ABOVE *Granite and marble are perfect for creating precise, geometric patterns. Here, the jewel-like quality of red and black granites suits the sharpness of the motif and emphasizes the white circle against the black marble floor.*

OPPOSITE *The simple strength of this plain granite floor matches the confident practicality of the kitchen's plain brickwork and stainless-steel equipment. Like all the elements in this interior, the floor is unselfconscious and appropriate.*

Terrazzo

Terrazzo was developed many centuries ago as a more versatile and economic substitute for marble or granite slabs. It consists of a wet mixture of marble or other stone chippings in a cement or cement-epoxy base, which can be formed into tiles, moulded panels or shapes, such as stair treads, to be laid dry onto the floor. It is also possible to lay the wet mixture directly onto a concrete floor, but this is an expensive and specialist job and is rarely done today in domestic interiors although it was a common feature of buildings in the 1930s. The polished surface has a mottled mosaic effect, either bold with large chippings, or more delicate with smaller finer flecks. The colour range includes the full spectrum of marbles. The cement base can also be coloured, either to contrast with the stone chips or to blend with them.

Terrazzo is extremely durable. The tiles are pre-ground and do not need finishing after laying, while terrazzo laid wet *in situ* requires grinding and polishing with special machinery. Terrazzo laid *in situ* requires expansion joints at 1m (around 3ft) intervals and should only be installed by a skilled professional.

Laying terrazzo *in situ* offers unusual opportunities for a designer, as when wet it can be formed into any three-dimensional shape, following contours. It has a rather tough, muscular quality, but in bespoke construction can be used to exciting effect on curves and up walls, a kind of application that was much favoured in the 1930s. In such cases, the layer of marble chippings should be about 6mm (¼in) deep, and the overall thickness no less than 25mm (1in).

Terrazzo tiles are usually 10mm (⅜in) thick and in most situations will last as long as stone. Tiles come in a range of sizes, ranging from the standard 30×30cm (11¾×11¾in) to 40×40cm (15¾×15¾in), 60×40cm (23½×15¾in) and 60×60cm (23½×23½in). Terrazzo floors are very heavy and can be laid safely only on a sand and cement screed on concrete. For laying terrazzo tiles follow the normal thick-bed method described on page 178.

Selection & Design

All stone floors are practical. Easy to maintain, they will continue to look good or even improve with age, and they will never need replacing. Except in a kitchen, the choice of stone will be made mainly on aesthetic grounds, and while there are many aspects to consider, two are of overriding importance. Choose a stone appropriate to the context in which it will be laid, and a colour and pattern of laying that do not dominate the room. Pay attention to the way that the stone relates to the period and style of the building. Even if a house has no other stone element, the floor needs to be appropriate to the period and location. It should either feel part of the history of the building or be a clear and

In this beautiful hotel room in Goa, a pattern of stars on a blue background brings a welcome coolness in the tropical heat, while the reflective quality of the floor casts a watery light deep into the interior.

The brass joint strips needed in the casting of large areas of terrazzo are perfectly integrated with the rest of the design, their sheen adding to the sparkle of the shimmering stars.

ABOVE *The most elegant and intricate patterns can be created by using a bush hammer on limestone. This technique can also be applied to dry concrete. Changes in surface texture offer considerable design opportunity within a single overall material.*

uncompromisingly modern contrast. You could, for example, in an old rough walled room, set smoothly polished travertine in steel frames so that it does not touch the old walls, to provide an interesting counterpoint of textures.

Polished marble suggests opulence and sophistication and is, perhaps, slightly exotic. Granite is elegant, but less exotic than marble. Tough, solid and secure, it is the stuff of which castles are built. Lime- or sandstone is also elegant but not showy, discreetly modish with a simple glowing warmth. Probably the most ruggedly handsome, solid and sensible, with a strong feel of indigenous architecture, are slate and sandstones such as York stone, particularly when they are laid in large flags.

The extent of the stone surface – whether it is used as a whole floor or in limited areas – will affect our response to the space. Extensive ground-floor spaces, either large rooms or knocked-through open-plan areas, look very attractive laid with large flagstones. This gives the impression that the floor is an original part of the building, particularly if the stones are laid to run through doorways into the areas beyond.

Selecting the right size of tile or slab is important. Regularly shaped machine-cut tiles will be read unconsciously as a thin, non-structural overlay, while large flags will seem to be integral to the structure. If you are trying to keep a traditional feel, flags are preferable to smaller machined tiles, which are a more recent product. In older country properties – manor houses, farmhouses or cottages – the ground floor is likely to have been built with flags of the local stone. This does not apply to the grandest country houses, however, whose owners could afford the latest fashion in imported stone, bringing York stone to London, or Italian marble to Connecticut or Georgia. Marble is an exception to the rule that thin tiles are modern, as the Italian marble used for grand floors in the eighteenth and nineteenth centuries was imported in the form of relatively thin slabs.

Light and reflectivity are important factors in selecting a stone. This is one reason why limestone has become popular as the fashion has developed for airy, clear interiors. In rooms where the floor should not compete for visual attention with the rest of the furnishings, lime- and sandstones – rather like the lighter hardwoods – make visually quiet backgrounds, suitable for contemporary as well as traditional interior styles. However, in regions where it is indigenous, slate would be a more appropriate choice than imported stone, and slate has a wonderfully solid and satisfying feel.

Slate, marble and granite are also more suitable than the lighter stones for nineteenth-century Gothic revival houses. In this ornate, decorative style it is appropriate to combine stones, particularly those of darker colours: slate with bands or cabochons of white marble, or granite with coloured marble borders and inlay. Bespoke work of this kind is expensive, but it is possible to obtain pre-cut marble patterns for inlay. Designs based on paler palettes are often associated with grand Neoclassical houses and are more appropriate to Georgian and more classic period homes.

Marble inlaid patterns tend to be very powerful, and to dominate a room. They are perhaps best limited to sparsely furnished areas, such as entrance halls. Plain, lighter marbles are ideal for conservatories or garden rooms. Of course marble has been used traditionally in bath houses throughout the world, not only for floors, but for all surfaces. Elegant and luxurious, as well as practical and hygienic, it can create beautiful bathing areas. Care must be taken, however, to avoid too highly polished a surface, to minimize the risk of people slipping.

The traditional base for stone floors was natural earth, but today they are usually laid on concrete ground or upper floors, which are finished with a sand and cement screed as part of the building process. Tiles and slabs can be laid on timber floors but they are heavy, and you need to make sure that the timber structure is strong enough to accept the weight.

In many houses constructed or renovated in the twentieth century, screeds will have been laid on ground floors to allow for a relatively thin covering, such as quarry tiles, carpet or parquet, and you will have to take this into account if laying a stone floor. It may be necessary to restrict your choice to thin new stone or to take up the screed. This latter course is a major undertaking and should only be undertaken by a competent builder or flooring company. If, however, you are constructing a new concrete floor or replacing an old earthen or timber floor with a concrete one, you will have greater freedom of choice in the type and size of stone you use. You could also take the opportunity to install under-floor heating (see page 174).

BELOW This room confidently celebrates the beauty of a single material. Massive travertine slabs combine with a monumental bath, hewn out of a single piece of marble, and large waterspout to create an interior of truly heroic qualities. The clarity of the surfaces is emphasized by the crisp gap between floor and wall.

CERAMICS & FIRED EARTH

Since prehistoric times mankind has exploited the fact that soft muds can be transformed by fire into a substance as hard as stone. Ceramic tiles and household ware remain the most durable of all man-made products, surviving from almost every region and every century.

Clay floors – glazed or unglazed, tiles or bricks – are among the most versatile of all floorings. They are not only extremely durable but also provide a vast range of decorative possibilities, from extravagant colours and complex glazed patterns to the precise geometry of quarry tiles or the primitive rusticity of hand-made terracotta. It is not surprising that tiles continue to have such universal appeal: the tiled floor you lay will not only serve and delight during your lifetime, but might be in place hundreds of years from now.

Although the earliest domestic floors were made simply of stamped earth and mud, the growth in the number of permanent buildings and the hygiene requirements of increasing populations led to the introduction of more hard-wearing surfaces that would be easier to keep clean. Since stone was expensive, hard to work and not always available, the simple technique of baking earth for use as floor tiles evolved throughout Europe and Asia many centuries ago. In the Americas, despite an advanced ceramic vessel and figure tradition, there seems to have been little use of clay tiles until the arrival of the Spanish in the sixteenth century. The application of glazes is thought to have originated in Egypt or Mesopotamia, where copper oxides were first used to produce the characteristic turquoises and blues.

Earthenware floor tiles were made in Northern Europe from early medieval times, using locally obtained red-brown to cream clays, glazed with a limited palette of greys and greens derived from iron and copper. At around the same time, craftsmen in the East were using a wide range of glaze compounds to develop a much richer and brighter palette, seen in the decoration of Islamic

These hand-made terracotta tiles are a fine example of the timeless simplicity of ceramic flooring at its best – mellow, with gently varied colour and subtle texture. Here, these qualities are reflected in the colour and texture of the wooden wall beyond. The interior furnishings, made of crisply modern metal but to traditional design, are set off by this plain and undemonstrative floor with its narrow terracotta skirting tiles and the band of pebbles inset in the doorways.

mosques from Central Asia right across to Moorish Spain. The extraordinary richness of the Moorish, Persian and Eastern decorative tradition demonstrates the art of decorative glazed tiling at its most advanced.

The sixteenth and seventeenth centuries saw a gradual mingling and cross-fertilization of the decorative styles of East and West, due to wider trading links and better communications. When the Moorish craftsmen were expelled from Spain in this period they took their skills to other parts of Europe, helping to disseminate the fashion for brilliant glazes. At about the same time, the development of a polychrome (multicoloured) lustreware, known as majolica, in the Italian town of Faenza created a fashion for ornate and colourful ceramics. The cultured and wealthy throughout Europe decorated the floors and walls of their houses with heraldic, geometric and wildlife designs in turquoises, greens and yellows on backgrounds of tin white. Inspiration for blue and white ceramic ware came from the Far East, a style developed by the Dutch Delftware industry. The domestic interiors painted by Vermeer and De Hooch in the seventeenth century show blue and white vases, vessels and tiles used as skirting boards and in fireplaces.

The industrial revolution transformed traditional hand-crafted ceramics and made cheap multicoloured ceramic decoration available in vast quantities to the middle classes. But by the late nineteenth century there was a reaction against the lack of variety in mass-produced ceramics, prompting a return to hand production by European designers such as William Morris, William De Morgan and Walter Crane, and in America H.C. Mercer. On both sides of the Atlantic small hand-production workshops were set up which had a considerable influence on ceramic decoration, mainly in the Art Nouveau style.

From the 1920s decorative ceramic production declined under the influence of the modernist movement, which rejected the decorative flourishes of the Art Nouveau and Art Deco eras in favour of plainer, more functional surfaces. Today however, this purism has given way to a culture in which all styles are acceptable and tiles are again being appreciated as one of the most versatile of flooring materials. To take just one example, the ubiquitous restoration of Victorian houses has led to a demand for encaustic tiles, with a consequent growth in the number of companies supplying them in an extensive range of colours and patterns.

ABOVE *These glazed antique Italian floor tiles with their two different approaches to pattern demonstrate the versatility of ceramic flooring. The bold blue and yellow tiles at the top are set as a band in grey to form a strong feature. Laid over the whole floor, they would create a powerful diagonal effect. The simple green and blue repeating leaves of the tiles below make a subtle all-over pattern, which can be made to appear regular by laying all the tiles in the same direction, or more random by varying the direction as here.*

Tile Manufacture

One of the commonest materials of the earth's crust, clay is essentially ground and compressed rock, combined with water and traces of various minerals. These include feldspar, a silicate used in the manufacture of glass. Clay is obtained by simply digging it out of the ground, and its appearance differs because of the variety of minerals and impurities in different regions, hence the varied and localized character of traditional tiles and bricks. The presence of iron oxide, for example, gives the familiar reddish-brown colour to terracotta clay. In mass production, different clays are invariably mixed together, resulting in a uniform product of regular size, shape and texture.

Clay is naturally malleable, and while wet can be formed into any shape.

When allowed to dry it hardens and becomes brittle, but remains fragile. Heating in a kiln releases water and produces a substance that increases in hardness and durability as the temperature rises. When clay is fired to above 900°C (1652°F) it gains strength but remains porous, and is known as low-fired or earthenware. Terracotta tiles are produced in this way; like low-fired house-bricks, they will decay rapidly when used externally and are vulnerable to damage by frost. At temperatures above 900°C (1652°F) the feldspar begins to fuse into a glass-like substance, until at approximately 1180°C (2156°F) the clay becomes totally impervious to water, staining and frost damage. Tiles fired to this state, which include quarry and encaustic tiles (see pages 54 and 56), are known as vitrified, from the Latin word *vitrum*, meaning glass. Fully vitrified tiles can be left unglazed, while low-fired earthenware tiles, because of their porosity, need to be either glazed or sealed to make them impervious to water. Encaustic or quarry tiles are usually suitable for external use, but you should check this with the manufacturer.

As well as the raw materials and firing temperature, the method of manufacture will also greatly affect the character of ceramic tiles. Traditionally, tiles were formed by hand, with the clay either rolled out into sheets and cut to shape, or squeezed into box moulds. While drying, the tiles would naturally shrink and deform, giving the surface and shape a hand-worked quality and ensuring that each tile was unique. Machine-made tiles are extruded in uniform thickness, size, colour and texture, and are therefore identical unless variety is purposefully introduced in the moulds. Tiles fired in traditional kilns with erratic heat sources, such as timber, have a natural variation of colour and texture, while the gas or electric kilns used in mass production eliminate these subtle variations. Craft potters today still prefer wood-burning kilns, and more expensive wood-fired tiles are available from small studio potteries.

A glaze not only makes porous tiles waterproof but affords the opportunity to introduce a whole world of colour and pattern by means of surface decoration. Glazing materials are composed of mineral compounds, including silica, which are ground and then mixed with water and applied to the tile. When heated, the compounds fuse together into a molten substance that cools to form a layer of glass. The glass-forming compounds use a wide range of oxides, can be clear, opaque or coloured, and produce gloss or matt finishes. Glaze is usually applied to a tile that has been fired once to a relatively low temperature (a biscuit tile). The tile is then fired again. On low-fired earthenware the glaze remains essentially a separate layer, which is subject to damage and can wear off, as can be seen on many old tiles. At higher temperatures the glaze bonds with the body of the tile, making it more durable and frost-proof. Most glazed tiles are suitable for use on floors, although abrasion will eventually cause wear on softer tiles.

Of the three main methods generally used for applying glazing compounds, the most traditional, which is appropriate for finely detailed hand-painted decoration, involves painting the tile with coloured oxides. These are then over-glazed with a transparent glaze, usually lead-based. For broad areas of colour and larger-scale decoration, the glaze solution itself – usually tin-based – is coloured and applied. A layer of coloured clay can also be applied in very liquid form called 'slip', the colours of which tend to be limited to the earthy creams, reds and browns of natural clays.

BELOW *Hand-painted 'antiqued' tiles with a delicate slip decoration are covered in a clear glaze suitable for wet areas. The recessive joints allow the delicate colouring and decoration to stand out.*

FAR BELOW *This simple tiling grid is almost a mosaic. The tiles are in complementary colours intensified by the thick glaze and given additional appeal because of their uneven nature. Depth is further emphasized by the black inserts at the intersections, whose shapes echo Moorish forms.*

Terracotta Tiles

Terracotta simply means 'baked earth'. These tiles are unglazed, medium-fired and therefore relatively porous. They derive their colour from the clay from which they are made, giving them a rich, warm, natural appearance, ranging from pale, almost yellow clays, shot through with pink, through variegated red-oranges and red-browns, to deeper reds. Some are made by hand, others by differing degrees of mechanization, and they are available in many shapes and sizes. A well-laid and polished terracotta floor can offer attractive variations in colour and texture and provide a calm background for any furnishing style. Sometimes known as 'pammets', hand-made, wood-fired tiles have a beautiful rustic quality. Some manufacturers try to simulate the appearance of wear and age by distressing each tile. If you are determined to create a well-worn, historic feel, look for old reclaimed tiles which are now being imported from Europe.

New terracotta tiles come in a variety of shapes and sizes, but most suppliers

OPPOSITE *All of these terracotta tiles, whether new or reclaimed, are hand-made and provide their own variety of colour and texture. Laid in a number of different patterns, with only discreet use of inserts, such as slate key squares or oak strips, they demonstrate the rich and fascinating options available even in a single material.*

BELOW *The unpolished roughness of these uneven reclaimed terracotta tiles is entirely appropriate for the simple, thick, uneven walls of this old cottage.*

offer squares of 30cm (11¾in), 25cm (just under 10in) or 20cm (just under 8in), or hexagons in a range of sizes which can be used on their own or combined with square tiles to form a variety of patterns. Some manufacturers also make 30.5cm (12in) squares for sale in America. Tiles are generally between 17mm (¾in) and 22mm (⅞in) thick. Larger hand-made tiles can be up to 40cm (15¾in) square, and some manufacturers also provide tiles 10cm (4in) square or smaller for borders and insets.

If you plan to use second-hand tiles remember that size will depend on what the importer has been able to find. As terracotta tiles are porous, they need sealing to avoid permanent staining and water absorption. Sealing and maintenance are discussed on page 65.

BELOW LEFT *The calm warmth and richness of this interior is created by the use of the same two colours of smooth, machine-made terracotta tiles running through a sequence of rooms, with a simple change of tile direction at edges and doorways. The bands around the edges allow the chequerboard to read because they use only one colour. The contrasting grey-green of the walls adds to the serenity of the whole.*

OPPOSITE *Hand-made terracotta tiles fired in a traditional kiln display all the variety of tone and texture of old tiles. The joints are so wide they almost form a tartan pattern, and their even tone offsets the variety in the tiles as well as leaving their attractive irregular edges exposed.*

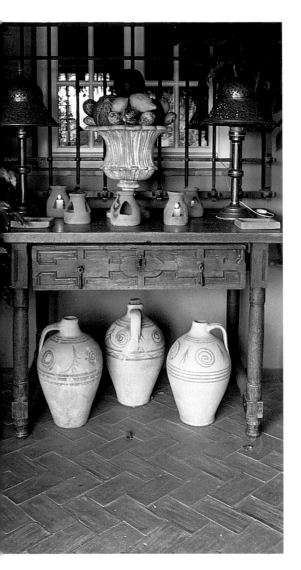

Bricks

Bricks combine the durability of quarry tiles with the rustic quality of terracotta. Flooring bricks are usually called pavers (or paviors). They are fired to higher temperatures and are therefore denser than most walling bricks. Normal walling bricks can be used internally. They measure 21.5×10.2×6.5cm (9×4½×3in). Pavers are the same width and length but vary between 3 and 5cm (1½ and 2in) deep.

Flooring bricks are produced in the same way as terracotta tiles, and the colours available are within the same earthy red-brown range, with some darker blues, greys and creams. They can be used to create an extremely strong and durable floor with a rugged feel, and are traditionally associated with utility rooms and working areas such as dairies, sculleries and cellars.

Bricks are difficult to clean, and you should avoid laying them in kitchens and bathrooms. Because of their size and weight it is sensible to consider brick only for ground floors and in spaces where you have sufficient depth. Together with the thick concrete slab and screed required to support it, a new brick floor will require a minimum depth of around 27.5cm (11in). Bricks can be laid with staggered joints, as in a wall, in groups of three to form squares, or in patterns such as Catherine wheel or herringbone. To seal them you can use either silicone sealers or polyurethane varnishes.

Quarry Tiles

Quarry tiles, which derive their name from the Old French *quarré*, meaning square, are machine-made, regular, dense, vitrified and therefore impervious. They were developed in the nineteenth century for industrial premises and their use is still widespread where a tough, impermeable ceramic surface is needed. Because they are machine-made they tend to have a very uniform appearance and some manufacturers deliberately introduce flashes of colour or variegation to alleviate this.

Quarry tiles come in a range of earthy reds and browns, charcoal greys and blacks, very dark blues and creams. Sizes are standard and usually 15cm (6in) square by 9 or 12mm (⅜ or ½in) thick, but a limited range of other sizes and half-tiles is available. As a legacy of their industrial origins there is an extensive range of accessories – corners, skirtings, skirting angles, safety raised studded tiles, stair nosings and channels. Use of these accessories can create a tough modern feel, and the studded tiles are particularly useful in places that get very wet, such as showers, utility rooms or swimming pools. Their precise shape forms a background with a strong geometric quality which looks particularly good in cream.

Quarry tiles are very versatile and they can be used to create a simple classic chequerboard or combined with other materials to form interesting patterns. In many respects their precise, flat quality is similar to that of encaustic tiles. Although quarry tiles can become dull with particularly hard wear, manufacturers do not advise using any kind of finish on them. Polishes tend to collect more dirt than the tile.

ABOVE *Laid in a simple herringbone pattern, bricks have been used here to make a hard-wearing floor with a rugged appearance complemented by the solid wooden table. The joints between bricks are attractively tight and the smooth texture of the floor surface reflects the light.*

OPPOSITE *A simple chequerboard of diagonal quarry tiles gives this kitchen a functional appearance which is also traditional and elegant. The red and cream tiles add warmth and colour to the pale timber fitted cupboards, the glass and chrome of the sink area and the neutral shades of the unusual chairs and table.*

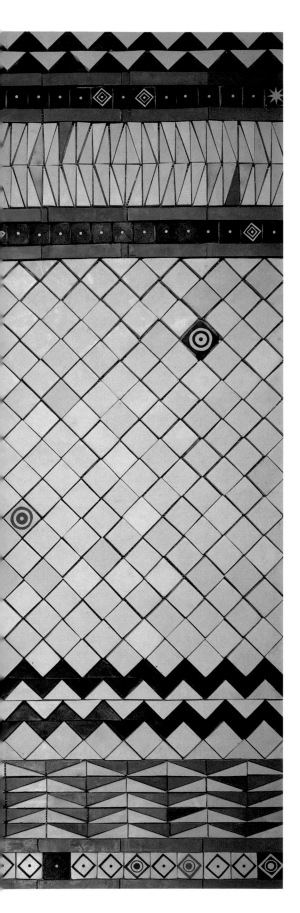

Encaustic Tiles

These patterned, machine-made tiles are fired with the design formed in the body of the tile, a process developed in the early nineteenth century. Encaustic tiles are made by pressing powdered clay compound into moulds, and the patterns are usually produced by indenting a shape on the surface, which is then filled with clay slip before firing. Encaustic tiles tend to be smaller than most – 7.5cm or 10cm (3in or 4in) square, with matching halves, narrow border tiles and diagonal insets. They were mass produced and became very fashionable during the nineteenth century, when their strong, inexpensive decorative potential was widely exploited. The Victorian decorative extravagance made possible by newly industrialized manufacturing processes can be seen at its best in floors such as those at Osborne House on the Isle of Wight and at architect Sir Charles Barry's House of Commons, London. Production of encaustic tiles dwindled to virtually nothing in the early twentieth century, but the growth in the restoration of Victorian houses has prompted a revival in their manufacture.

Some modern encaustic tiles are made of powdered stone and marble mixtures which are then coloured, giving a slightly softer edge to the patterns where the coloured slips and oxides merge into the body of the tile. Developed as a less expensive substitute for clay, these are generally made in Morocco.

A few small producers have developed delightful hand-stencilled designs and these tiles combine durability and imperviousness with the character of hand decoration. While they are relatively expensive, they present an alternative to the more common tin-glaze decorated tiles. They generally come in larger sizes than traditional encaustic tiles, and can be commissioned as single tiles or as panels forming a unified design. Individual tiles of this kind can be used successfully as accents in a plain floor or to create borders. Because the patterns are formed with clay slips, the colours tend to be from a natural palette of greys, blues, reds and creams, which lend a calm and sophisticated quality to a floor.

LEFT AND RIGHT *Encaustic tiles can be used to provide a single bold motif, such as a sunburst, or combined to create a kind of ceramic carpet based on contrasting colours and shapes. The striking panel on the left is built of squares, rectangles and triangles of different sizes. Its interplay of circles and straight lines, waves and stripes, carries stylistic echoes of the decorative work of the Viennese painter, Gustav Klimt.*

OPPOSITE *Old encaustic tiles in a range of muted colours are laid to form an all-over pattern with borders in this spacious kitchen, where the traditional idiom predominates.*

Glazed Tiles

Glazed floor tiles come in every conceivable colour, pattern and shape, and used imaginatively they can be as extravagantly colourful or sophisticatedly subtle as you wish. Plain areas of glaze applied thickly can seem like pools of colour, glowing with a rich warmth – an impression much sought after at the end of the nineteenth century when they were especially popular. Given the range of sizes and shapes available, the possibilities for developing patterns and decorative themes are limitless. You should beware, however, of buying on impulse. Before visiting the many tile showrooms with their countless enticing displays, it is wise to formulate a clear, overall design concept based on the quality and feel of the floor you wish to create. Colour and pattern need to be planned as a co-ordinated whole for floor, furniture and walls. Remember that the more powerful your tiling decoration, the more restricted your choice will be with regard to other design elements.

Decorated floor tiles can be attractive when used as skirtings, or as insets among other kinds of tile, such as terracotta. They can also be combined to match or complement wall tiling. Although glazed floor tiles may look the same as wall tiles, they need to be stronger and thicker, and are usually 9–12mm (⅜–½in) thick. In some areas they may present a problem because they are potentially slippery, especially when wet.

OPPOSITE *Reclaimed glazed bricks set in a plain brick patio create a focus beneath a table. The bricks form a rug-like motif not only by virtue of their strong colours, but by their double herringbone pattern which contrasts with the single herringbone of the plain bricks. The use of bricks here underlines the dual nature of a space linking indoors with outdoors.*

BELOW *The high gloss on these glazed tiles gives a cool, shimmery quality to the room, which is emphasized by their sea-green colour. The elaborate two-colour pattern demonstrates what can be achieved with interlocking shapes.*

BELOW *This room is designed to have an informal feeling indicating the insertion of the bathroom into an older, grander space. This feeling is emphasized by the use of decorated tiles in an informal, scattered way and by running the pattern under the bath.*

OPPOSITE *Hand-made pale blue tiles with a gentle variety of tones create a calm, elegant floor. A touch of colourful interest is provided by the patterned tiling set around the foot of the pillar, in which different tones of blue are combined with yellowy brown.*

Porcelain Stoneware Tiles

A relatively new ceramic flooring material, porcelain stoneware is made almost exclusively in Italy. Porcelain is clay with a high kaolin content, and is fired at higher temperatures than any other ceramic material. It is consequently highly vitrified and impervious, which is why it was traditionally used for fine crockery. The high firings allow the inclusion of a large proportion of natural oxides and feldspar mineral, and create a very strong material. Porcelain stoneware tiles are not decorated, but are made in a range of colours and surfaces that closely emulate natural stones and terrazzo. They are a very good and economic substitute for granite. They are available in matt or gloss, in squares varying from 25mm (1in) square for use as mosaic up to 60cm (24in) square and in thicknesses of 12 or 15 mm (½ and ⅝in).

The very precise and even nature of porcelain tiles makes them ideal for forming geometric patterns. Variation and interest can be introduced by simply changing the size of the tiles, the direction in which they are laid, the jointing pattern or the use of smaller square tiles laid in a row or two to form a border round a field of larger tiles. The hard-wearing and easy maintenance properties of porcelain tiles means that they are a good choice for ground-floor entrance halls and kitchens. However, their very smooth precise quality gives these floors a rather austere, formal quality. Without compensating soft furnishings and colours they may create a rather cold atmosphere.

Selection & Design

Ceramics can be used to create almost any style, from the rustic to the geometrically precise, from the homely to the palatial, and from the restful to the dazzling. Because of their durability and their resistance to water, staining or heavy use, tiles are ideally suited to areas such as bathrooms, kitchens, utility rooms and entrance halls, where the floor will become wet or be regularly washed. However, they are inflexible, and if you are contemplating a tiled floor you should remember that they will have to be laid on a flat and stable base. Even on a solid timber floor, you will probably need to add a plywood base to ensure that the surface is completely flat. Full instructions for laying and bedding tiles are on pages 176–79.

When choosing the colour of your tiles, bear in mind the dirt factor. Cleaning will be a continual problem if you use light colours in a garden or utility room, where muddy boots and family pets come and go. A more practical option might be a darker colour, which could perhaps be brightened with some inlaid coloured tiles, or a geometric pattern of mixed creams and blues or greys. A bathroom, however, where outdoor mud is unlikely to penetrate, can be given a clean crisp appearance with tiles in lighter colours and whites.

By and large, the earthy reds, browns and greys of low-fired tiles are associated with natural, unsophisticated interiors, while the brighter high-fired azures, cobalts and greens which were once only available at centres of wealth and technical advance suggest a more artistic refinement. Terracotta tiles, for example, with their warm simplicity, are ideal for a farmhouse kitchen or dining

BELOW *A collection of encaustic tiles shows the variety of colours and designs now available, ranging from simple geometrical to stylized floral patterns. These large tiles are formed on a concrete core and are often produced in North Africa.*

OPPOSITE *Simple glazed tiles create a sumptuous bathing area. The warm cream hand-made tiles are delicately framed by blue and cream scrollwork tiles with an oriental feel. The floor is differentiated from the walls by its wide blue joints, which add pattern while minimizing slipperiness.*

room. By contrast, for a more elaborate decorative look, patterned encaustic tiles or coloured quarries based on Victorian designs can be used to give the colour of rugs but with the durability and economy of machine-made ceramics. They are particularly suitable for adding interest to smaller areas such as entrance halls, passages or utility rooms.

A regular grid of plain tiles will look clean and modern, providing a perfect background for more elaborate rugs and furniture. Variation and interest can be introduced by simply changing the size of the tiles or the direction in which

BELOW *Green glazed bricks laid in bands and zig-zags contrast with plain unglazed clay bricks to make a bold and attractive staircase. Special clay nosings create a strong edge to each step, protect the green bricks from damage and make the surface less slippery.*

they are laid, or by combining ceramics with other materials. Contrasting or decorative inserts can be attractive when used as part of an all-over geometrical design. Cabochons are readily available in a wide range of colours and sizes to co-ordinate with larger tile sizes: they can be plain terracotta, glazed tiles or different materials such as slate or marble. The directional emphasis of these inserts can be used positively to complement the shape of the space. If you decide to use glazed inserts with unglazed tiles, the inserts should be laid so that they are slightly recessed to minimize wear on the glazed surface.

Other materials can be combined with ceramics equally well. To take one example, a tartan grid of terracotta alternating with narrower slate or even timber bands creates a subtle and sophisticated look. Marble can also be used this way for a grander effect, but it is important when mixing materials to maintain a careful balance between plain grounds and figured decoration, so as to avoid visual confusion. Remember, too, when combining different kinds of materials that they should be compatible in terms of their durability and maintenance.

Sealing & Maintenance

Ceramic tiles are one of the most maintenance-free materials. Non-porous ceramics such as quarry tiles, glazed tiles, porcelain and encaustic tiles should not be sealed or polished – nothing will be absorbed into the surface and any polishes will simply become slippery and absorb dirt.

Porous low-fired terracotta tiles should be sealed using boiled linseed oil or a proprietary sealant. Apply one coat to the surface and edges prior to laying and grouting in order to keep them clean. Once grouted apply a further coat to the whole of the floor. The oil or sealant will soak into the tiles, and if it does so quickly and becomes fully matt, a further application is warranted. Apply evenly using a soft cloth formed into a pad – uneven absorption can leave the tiles looking streaky. Any excess oil that has not been absorbed after 15–20 minutes should be wiped off. Leave the tiles for at least four hours, or ideally overnight, before applying a coat of floor wax. Two or three coats of wax are required initially, followed by further coats at weekly intervals for the first month to build up a hard-wearing surface.

Once they have been laid and sealed, tiled floors simply need sweeping with a soft broom and washing with warm water containing a neutral or low-sulphate detergent. Do not sprinkle the detergent on the floor, but dilute it first and always use it according to the manufacturer's instructions. On dirty floors leave the floor wet for up to ten minutes for the detergent to work and then mop away, repeating if necessary.

Removal of obstinate grease spots requires a little more care. On glazed tiles use a high alkaline detergent or one containing organic solvents. On unglazed tiles scrubbing the stain carefully with an abrasive cleaner should usually suffice. If not, try diluted bleach or pumice blocks. Always rinse your tiled floor thoroughly, and do not use soap on floors as this will leave a slippery film.

BELOW *Designed to emphasize the unusual basin fitting, these glazed tiles pick up the green in the walls to create an impression of minty freshness. The white and green chequerboard pattern with dark joints is of the same early modern period style as the basin.*

MOSAIC

A mosaic is made of small pieces of stone, glass or ceramic – still known by the Latin term *tesserae* – set into a base. The techniques of mosaic can also be used to assemble many other kinds of hard material into a picture or pattern, and designers today use a wide variety of objects, such as shells, broken ceramics or any small components. Modern production methods have allowed a range of patterns and designs to be manufactured in preformed sheets, which can be laid side by side like tiles to cover large areas or to form borders. However, the true virtue of mosaic lies in the opportunities it offers to create your own tailor-made floor designs, from the simple to the ornate, or to commission individual works of art of great richness and complexity.

Mosaics have been a central feature of palaces and temples throughout the world for thousands of years, and the finest examples of this ancient craft have long been objects of admiration and emulation. Because they are extremely durable, in many instances mosaic floors are all that remain of the great buildings of the past. In Greece, for example, floors of pebbles interspersed with iron strips have survived from around 1600 BC. These have a restrained palette reflecting the colour of the local stone, with backgrounds of white or grey and designs in dark reds, yellows, greens and black. Plain black and white geometric patterns were common.

Around the third century BC, the Romans began to produce small coloured ceramic tesserae, enabling the creation of smoother and more practical mosaics for indoor floors, and facilitating much more detailed and figurative designs. Images of mythological figures, animals and feasts adorn Roman domestic and public buildings from Britain to North Africa. Some of the best examples of these can still be seen in the pavemented floors of Pompeian houses and among the hundreds of villas excavated in mainland Britain. A popular and intriguing design (suitable for an eating area) was a trompe l'oeil representation of the unswept leftovers of a feast.

Richly coloured tesserae made from opaque glass, known as smalti, were developed by Byzantine artists living in Venice around 400-600 AD. Their brilliant colours and high gloss led to an explosion of creativity, combining the stylistic features of the West with the Eastern love of surface decoration. The smalti mosaics in the church of San Vitale in Ravenna, the last Imperial capital of Italy, represent the culmination of this technique and show the sumptuous colour and intricate designs of the craft at its most developed.

This modern mosaic deliberately emulates the incomplete and broken forms of antique examples unearthed by archaeologists. Its ancient design with a central emblem and Greek key pattern border accords with the Corinthian pilasters and cornice and provides an appropriate complement to the false fresco on the walls of the room. All elements in this room are coordinated to create a theatrical effect.

The use of mosaic declined in Europe from the fourteenth century, although it remained a feature of ecclesiastical design during the next few hundred years, as can be seen in the decoration of St Peter's in Rome. Towards the end of the nineteenth century, the Victorian fascination for the exotic and eclecticism brought a revival of interest in the technique on both sides of the Atlantic, and this has continued to the present day. New mosaics can be costly because they are labour-intensive, but you can use combinations of designs available in pre-fabricated sheets to install a beautiful and long-lasting floor with little time and effort and at a fraction of the cost of commissioning an original work from an artist specializing in mosaic work.

A mosaic floor will impart a historical, perhaps Mediterranean mood to a room. Its small, usually shiny pieces give it a rich vitality, and the skill required to lay it suggests a luxury generally associated with places of grandeur. Mosaic patterns, such as scrolls, spirals and interlocking circles, and even plain-coloured mosaics – which are in fact never plain, being built up of so many small and subtly different pieces – tend to attract the eye and feel busy. Traditionally, therefore, rooms with mosaic floors have been adorned with very little furniture. In living rooms, where you may want your floor to be visually quieter, the powerful effect of mosaic might be best deployed to form an ornate but narrow border or as key square insets within a plainer material such as tiles, slabs of marble or a neutral-coloured stone. This combination of plain and patterned areas can look particularly good in formal rooms or as a feature in a hallway. Mosaics are also ideal for use on steps as they can be laid on both vertical and horizontal surfaces. Whatever the extent or pattern of your mosaic, careful lighting is very important. Sidelighting positioned as low as possible shows up the surface texture best.

OPPOSITE ABOVE *Mosaics such as these, which appear elaborate, can be made comparatively easily from preformed patterned and plain designs supplied on a backing.*

OPPOSITE BELOW *The slightly washed-out colours and the matching of the beige mosaic to the surrounding slabs gives a subtle ancient quality to the floor.*

LEFT *Mosaic can be inserted as decorative motifs into other types of flooring as well as being used to create an overall pattern. Here the restrained use of rich red mosaic to form key squares adds interest and an underplayed opulence to the regularity of the stone slabs. The combination of plain squares and mosaic is repeated in more elaborate fashion in the decorative wall frieze, which is made of tesserae the same size as those in the floor.*

ABOVE *These purpose-made ceramic interlocking shapes form an endlessly fascinating geometric pattern of typically Moorish form and colour which can be repeated indefinitely either as a border or as an overall field.*

Materials & Methods

Traditionally tesserae are made by snipping small pieces from large sheets of marble, ceramic or glass. Some manufacturers produce tesserae formed in moulds, which are less expensive than the hand-made ones. They vary enormously in size but a range of 5–10mm (¼–⅜in) square gives the necessary small scale to form traditional images and designs. Larger pieces can be used to create more abstract designs and patterns. Pebbles and seashells, broken crockery and metal scrap can be collected from a number of sources and used as they are.

The basic techniques of mosaic-making have scarcely changed in the three to four thousand years since they were originally developed. The methods can be adapted to many materials, enabling you to develop your own ideas and make your floor as exciting and individual as you wish. Whatever you use, however, it is best to avoid pieces of any great depth since the size of the thickest piece will determine the thickness for the whole of the base of the floor, which will in turn affect doors, stairs, skirtings and fittings.

Mosaics can be formed by either the 'direct' or the 'indirect' method, depending on the nature of the material and the area to be covered. In the direct method the pieces are laid face upwards directly into the base as the floor is being laid. This technique is particularly useful where unusual materials such as pebbles or broken crockery are incorporated into the design, or where the design is very large. In the indirect method the tesserae are laid face down and in reverse onto a framed temporary support so that a layer of cement or resin can be poured to form a solid backing over the design, effectively forming a tile or panel which can be turned over and laid in the same way as a ceramic tile. Alternatively a water-soluble glue is used to bond the face of the tesserae arranged in their final design to sheets of strong paper, nylon mesh or hessian, which are then transported to the site and laid face outwards into wet cement. Once the cement has hardened, the facing can be removed with water. Indirect mosaics tend to be flatter and smoother than those laid directly into a base, which makes them particularly suitable for floors; but preventing the liquid backing from flowing onto the face requires considerable care.

To provide a tough, relatively smooth surface, the joints of mosaics laid on floors must be grouted. The basic techniques for grouting mosaics are the same as those used with ceramic tiles (see page 179). As the grout is brushed away the tesserae will be left slightly more elevated than the surface. It is also possible to lay a mosaic floor using commercially available panels of mosaic – combinations of plain and border tiles are available, usually approximately 20cm (8in) square and 19mm (¾in) thick, for laying on timber or solid floors.

OPPOSITE *A variety of different mosaics demonstrates the wide range of design options, whether you are using small hand-cut tesserae and smalti or larger more regular machine-made sheets of tesserae. Subdued shades reflecting the colours available in natural stone are suggestive of ancient mosaic work, as seen in the chequerboard at the bottom right, a detail from a domestic Roman pavement in Aquileia. Simple curved and linear border patterns and the circular wreath found on an area of exterior paving are based on classical designs. Brighter colours offer the possibility of creating more modern floors, both in wall-to-wall coverings and in many kinds of trompe l'oeil effects. The wavy lines of a mosaic 'rug' sit like fabric on the floor.*

Classic Design

The texture of a mosaic, like the texture of a painting, is an essential part of its appeal. As in a pointillist picture, what appear from a distance to be blocks of colour or gradations of tone break up into their individual elements when viewed from closer. The smaller the pieces of a mosaic, the finer the detail in the finished design. Unless factory-moulded materials are used, an essential characteristic of the medium is the subtle variation in size between each hand-cut piece which makes all tesserae unique.

Patterns and borders traditionally employed for mosaic work include repeatable motifs such as Greek key patterns, guilloches, scrolls and stylized floral motifs. Using smalti, pieces of brightly coloured ceramic or mirrors, you can create more modern geometric and colourful designs. The juxtaposition of small geometric shapes in bright colours, reminiscent of the Art Deco style, is particularly well suited to mosaic.

The Romans developed a number of ways in which tesserae can be arranged in a design. Some were based on two colours only and were thus relatively quick and easy to lay, which made them suitable for covering the floors of large-scale public buildings. Others, used principally in domestic interiors, required considerable skill and a multitude of colours to build up pictures of great vitality. An awareness of the different design possibilities may well influence the way you think about the patterns and images you wish to create.

Opus tesselatum and *opus regulatum* (literally 'work based on stone cubes and rules') are terms which describe an arrangement of more or less square tesserae in regular straight lines. If you buy tesserae in preformed tiles or sheets, this is how they are set out. Although perfect for constructing geometric shapes and for filling in the backgrounds to more complex motifs, this arrangement can look too regimented for figures and details.

Opus vermiculatum (literally 'worm-like work') is perhaps the most expressive and demanding form of mosaic-making. In designs with a central or repeated motif, the tesserae are laid in flowing lines which follow the shape of the image. Roman mosaics often feature several rows of *opus vermiculatum* in a motif and contrast this with a background composed of regular *opus tesselatum*. The outlines of the motif were usually drawn in a dark, contrasting colour to define the boundary between it and the background and to give the image clarity. To achieve the curves and colour nuances found in much of this work, the tesserae were of different shapes and sizes, and skilled mosaicists would often assemble the more complicated pictures and motifs in their own workshops to be installed as centrepieces in a larger floor. The more unusual technique of using fewer, larger shaped tesserae to build up an image is known as *opus sectile,* or 'work that can be cut'. This was employed when larger elements such as pieces of tile formed the tesserae.

Emblemata is the name given to central pictures or elaborate patterns set in a plain background. In Roman times such features were usually images of significance to the patron or location – a depiction of the patron saint of a church, for example, or scenes of hunting, fishing and harvesting. Central roundels, stars or polygons filled with geometric patterns are commonly found as emblemata on mosaic floors today.

BELOW *This example of elaborate mosaic work from a Roman villa in Aquileia combines* opus tesselatum *in the legs and background with* opus vermiculatum *to draw the halo and other detailed shapes. It demonstrates the mastery of rich detail achieved by ancient craftsmen. The vibrancy comes in large measure from the combination of surface texture with a muted palette of browns, creams and reds.*

Smalti & Glass

True smalti are pieces of coloured opaque glass, usually about 15×10×5mm (around ½×⅜×¼in) thick. They can be acquired in an almost infinite range of colours and create a beautiful effect of depth and luminosity. Traditionally one of the most prized materials for mosaics, smalti are hand-made, almost exclusively in Italy, and are therefore expensive. Because they are small and fairly irregular, they require considerable skill to work with but make the richest and most subtly varied of all mosaics.

Silver and gold smalti, a feature of the finest historical mosaics, are still available to mosaicists today, but at a price. Gold and silver leaf is sandwiched between two layers of plain glass, giving the tesserae a wonderfully lustrous quality. The cost of using such luxurious materials is obviously prohibitive in all but the smallest areas, but a few pieces can be incorporated into a larger design to introduce exciting highlights.

Machine-made glass tesserae are also obtainable. They come in a less extensive range of colours than smalti but cost much less. Because they are larger (usually 20×20mm (¾×¾in) square) and more regular, they are far easier to work with and can be obtained both loose or stuck down onto adhesive paper in panels. These are ideal for use in indirect method mosaics.

ABOVE *Brightly coloured smalti demonstrate a characteristic richness of colour and ability to reflect the light. Only a few tesserae of contrasting green are needed to enliven the pattern.*

LEFT *Scrolls of glistening gold smalti are sufficient to draw a powerful shape against the quieter background of subtly varied tesserae. These have been skilfully laid in a radial pattern to reinforce the lines of the smalti.*

Pebbles & Seashells

Pebbles are one of the simplest materials available for mosaic, and archaeological evidence shows that they have been used in floors since at least the time of Alexander the Great. Their natural variations in size and colour offer opportunities for creating beautiful and subtle harmonious patterns within a colour range of black, natural stone greys, whites and beiges. Pebbles are generally used in the direct method, pushed deeply into a base of cement, wet concrete or resin. They can also be laid in a dry sand and cement mixture and then hosed down to activate the mixture.

Seashells have also been traditionally used to create mosaics, particularly as ornamental features, and they make excellent highlights and accents when added to pebble floors. All but the most brittle shells can be used in the same ways as pebble, but it is best to ensure that the hollow undersides of the shells are completely filled with the cement backing when laying so that they do not break when trodden underfoot.

While pebble and shell mosaics have a powerful, rugged quality, they are not

OPPOSITE *Here the colour of a simple pebble border complements the sea-blue of the window frames and supplies a graphic focus to this bathroom floor, inspired by the white sand beaches of the Mediterranean. A double row of pebbles has been set directly into a concrete screed, which has then been sealed. By limiting the pebbles to a border, any discomfort underfoot is minimized. This is a relatively simple floor treatment providing a very durable, low-maintenance solution at minimum cost.*

ABOVE *In a tight-knit, classically inspired black-and-white design, this pebble mosaic floor boasts a double border of foliage tendrils framing a central emblema. The small pebbles, perfectly matched for size, follow the lines of the design in the patterned areas, but are set in straight lines to make the background.*

LEFT *An all-over field of white marble pebbles framed in a contrasting crenellated border of blue vitreous glass tesserae gives texture and visual interest to this hall floor.*

comfortable to walk on, especially in bare feet, unless packed closed together and pushed well down. However, they are durable, easily cleaned and highly resistant to slipping, and are therefore extremely practical in areas where wet footwear is likely to be worn, such as entrances and utility rooms. Seashells are a particularly appropriate and traditional material for bathrooms, and can be applied as a border around a more comfortable material such as tiles. Pebble and shell mosaics are perhaps the easiest type for the do-it-yourself enthusiast to experiment with, as the method of construction is so basic; and since the materials are themselves irregular in shape there is no loss of quality if joints and levels are somewhat uneven.

Ceramics & Other Materials

Pieces of ceramic tile or crockery can be used in exactly the same way as traditional stone or glass tesserae, and many artists today are creating floors with a variety of ceramic pieces that can justifiably be described as mosaics. The advantage of using ceramic is that a wide range of brilliant colours is available for very little cost. Pieces of scrap such as broken plates or cups can be used but are likely to have depth and so are most easily set into a cement bed. Any tesserae with rough edges, such as mirror, glass or metal, should be pressed deep into the base to prevent the edges causing injury. For more elaborate designs, the indirect method is also possible, allowing designs to be drawn out onto paper, the pieces laid out and glued face down and the whole pattern lifted into place. Provided the outward facing surface is relatively even, any size or shape of component can be included to form an unusual mosaic floor.

ABOVE AND RIGHT *These two contemporary mosaics show how broken tiles can be assembled into lively images. The contrast between the square tile above, broken and re-assembled almost into its original shape, and the randomly scattered segments around it, provides an intriguing interplay of forms suggestive of archaeological reconstruction. To form the head and feet of the turtle on the right, larger pieces of ceramic have been specially painted, while a strip of darker tesserae to the left of it creates the illusion of a shadow underneath.*

Practical Considerations

Once you have decided on a mosaic floor, and have some idea of the pattern and scale of your desired mosaic, you will need to consider how it is to be installed. Some simple designs, such as pebble mosaics, can be laid with a minimum of practice. Larger and more intricate designs using small tesserae are best left to the experts.

Most specialist companies will be able, within limits, to produce floors with patterns and shapes to match your design concept. But their standard designs using prefabricated sheets may be more practical and, since they are designed to minimize labour, less expensive than anything involving the direct method of installation. Patterns, borders and shapes of all descriptions are available in prefabricated form, as well as sheets of plain colours. The tesserae are usually made of ceramic or of coloured glass, similar to but less vibrant than smalti, and come in a fairly wide range of colours, some with veining to imitate marble. The individual pieces are usually about 20mm (¾in) square and about 4mm (⅛in) thick, machine-produced and precisely regular. The spaces between mass-produced tesserae are very uniform, giving the finished work a regularity not found in hand-laid mosaic work. Mosaics larger than 3m (10ft) in any one direction should incorporate expansion joints, the location of which needs to be considered in the design.

If you are thinking of commissioning a custom-made mosaic, bear in mind that it will be considerably more costly than a prefabricated design. Try to see the work of as many artists as you can *in situ*, and ensure that the artist you choose has a clear idea of your preferences from the outset. Depending on the size of the finished work and the method of construction used, professional mosaicists will either lay the floor in your home, or prepare designs in their own studios to be installed by themselves or by a specialist fixer.

Once the floor is in place, maintenance is comparatively easy. Traditional mosaic materials require no seal and will form an extremely durable and long-lasting floor covering. Surface dirt can be removed with a soft broom or a mop. Being washable and impermeable to stains, mosaic is particularly suitable for kitchens, entrances and bathrooms, and can even be extended up the sides of baths to provide a waterproof seal. Glass and ceramic mosaic may be slippery, but less so than polished stone or glazed tiles since the joints and the angled facets of the mosaic provide a textured and uneven surface. If one or two tesserae come loose, they can easily be rebedded with adhesive recommended by the layer.

Mosaics, particularly those made of pebbles, are fairly heavy, so should ideally be laid on a solid concrete sub-floor. The majority of mosaics are fixed to the floor with adhesives, but you will need to lay pebble mosaics in a sand and cement screed. This should be a mixture of one part cement to three parts sand and not less than 5cm (2in) thick, although the depth can vary to accommodate an uneven underlying surface. It is also possible to lay mosaic on timber floors covered with plywood (see page 177) using epoxy adhesives and grout, but the floor should be checked for strength before installing anything but the thinnest mosaic. The floor must also be entirely stable and even, so the mosaic does not crack once it is in place.

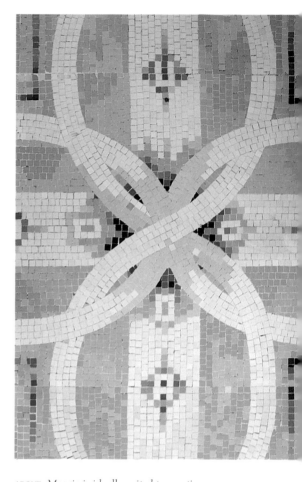

ABOVE *Mosaic is ideally suited to creating three-dimensional illusions of intertwining forms. Here the variation in colour and tone within the overall pattern gives subtlety and interest, while the irregularities contribute to the charm.*

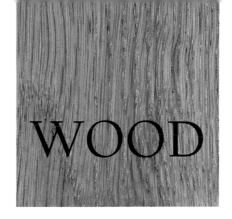

WOOD

There is perhaps no other material that creates such instant satisfaction as wood – so much so that when it is finely worked we are prompted to stretch out and feel it. Today, when our lives seem so mechanized and divorced from the natural world, the patina, texture and smell of wood convey the magic of nature, of trees and woodland groves.

In most temperate and tropical climates wood has until recently grown in abundance. It is strong, relatively light and portable, and is easily worked into simple or sophisticated forms. It is not surprising that wood has been one of the basic elements of building and flooring for centuries.

Wood can be divided into two broad types: hardwoods and softwoods. The hardwood deciduous trees growing in the temperate forests of Europe and America produce the lighter timbers such as oak, ash and maple. The evergreen broadleaf trees from tropical rainforests produce darker hardwoods, such as mahogany and teak. Softwoods, such as pine and cedar, are generally pale and grow in the mainly evergreen coniferous forests of Northern Europe, North America and Asia.

Traditionally, builders would have used whichever type of wood was available locally, whether they were constructing a palace or a cottage. Until the late seventeenth century in Europe and North America the most common woods for floors were oak and elm, with boards as wide as 40–50cm (16–20in). By the turn of the eighteenth century, however, the use of softwoods from the Baltic, such as Baltic fir, became common throughout Europe and the New World. In grand houses it was traditional for the edges of wooden floors in reception rooms to be stained or painted with elaborate patterns to frame a carpet. Even more sumptuous interiors boasted parquetry, a technique of making patterns from inset pieces of coloured woods developed from the marquetry of Italian cabinet makers. Hardwoods gradually became more and more expensive, and by the end of the nineteenth century only builders of the finest dwellings could afford hardwood for every floor, so it became common to use oak in the principal rooms and softwood on the upper floors. While softwood now accounts for the majority of new floors, mainly for economic reasons, hardwood is being increasingly used for overlay flooring. Composite boards such as plywood and chipboard are made from softwood.

The sparseness of the furnishings in this elegant room allows the hardwood boards with their diversity of colour and grain figuration to be fully appreciated, while the pale timber reflects the light from the full-length windows. The short lengths that form this prefinished plank system add to the interest of the floor, but the subtle variety in the wood in no way detracts from the beautiful lines and fine carving of the few carefully chosen pieces of furniture.

FROM TOP *These samples show the colours and grains of maple plank, beech plank, cherry strip and walnut strip.*

Choosing a Wood Floor

Both hardwoods and softwoods can be used throughout the house, although softwoods and hardwoods subject to moisture movement should be avoided in rooms such as bathrooms or kitchens where the floor regularly becomes wet, as the boards will degrade very quickly. This is why door sills, which are continually subject to weathering and abrasion, have traditionally been made from hardwood. When choosing your timber it is important to bear in mind the fundamental differences between the two types of wood. Hardwoods have a dense, closely grained and durable timber which is very resistant to damage and decay. Hardwood boards can have a lot of variation in grain pattern and colour, caused by changes in growth rates and the accumulation of layers within the tree. Softwoods grow faster and have a more regular open-grain structure. They are ideal for commercial forestry, are easier to work than hardwoods and thus more economic, but they are less durable.

The use of some tropical hardwoods is a controversial issue. The forests in which they grow play a vital part in the earth's ecosystem, but they are being cleared at an alarming rate, and the destruction of this natural resource is a cause for serious concern. The development in recent years of management regimes based on sustainable methods has meant that tropical hardwoods imported from these sources can still be used responsibly. But the ready availability of European and North American hardwoods provides an ample choice without resorting to tropical timbers. Some flooring companies stain these lighter hardwoods to look like tropical woods.

Each type of wood has its own characteristic grain pattern, colouring, feel and even scent, and it is these differences that will determine which wood you use for your floor. Oak and beech have marked flecks within the grain (known as trachoids), while ash or elm have a long wavy grain. Some pines have dark knots in their pale wood. A number of the more prolific timbers are sorted into grades, depending upon evenness of colour, knottiness and grain. Beech, for example, is available in clear, normal and flamy, the last being very knotty and the least expensive. Oak also comes in many grades

Light hardwoods, such as European beech, sycamore, American white oak and birch (in the form of birch-faced plywood), or the lighter softwoods, such as Norway spruce or silver fir, will give a bright feel to a room, while providing a neutral background for the striking display of colourful rugs and furniture. Yellower but still light are other softwoods, such as Scots pine (European redwood), Western white pine and Western hemlock, or hardwoods, such as ash and maple. For an orange-red tone choose American red oak, larch, cherry or Douglas fir; richer mid-brown timbers include English oak and elm, which will give a less stark, warmer feel. The darker oaks, walnuts or tropical hardwoods have a heavier more traditional quality, and will better withstand scratches and wear and tear.

Remember that all timbers, particularly the lighter ones and softwoods, will darken with age, becoming more yellow. Within each timber species the grain figuration can vary considerably, not only from tree to tree but according to the way the timber is cut. Therefore it is vital to see samples of the wood from the source you are considering using.

Timber Production

It is helpful to understand something of the production stages which affect the performance of timber when you are deciding which type of wood flooring to use. Timber is felled, cut into large sections, dried and then cut into smaller sections for specific uses. Logs are cut into sections in two ways, 'through and through' and 'quarter-sawn'.

While through-sawing can yield wide boards, the long edges of these boards are likely to bend upwards when the wood dries, an effect known as 'cupping'. Quarter-sawing results in narrower boards of better quality, but more wastage, so the timber is more expensive.

Drying or 'curing' is another crucial stage in timber production. The cells of freshly felled trees are full of wet sap, which must evaporate before the timber can be used. Traditionally timber was left to dry slowly until it had reached a stable moisture content, but this long and expensive process has been superseded for the most part by the use of large kilns. These dry timber quickly, but can cause considerable splitting and warping, particularly in hardwoods. Expensive air-dried timber is still used for the highest-quality floors, such as those in historic houses. Timber for use in buildings must have the correct moisture content and should be protected from adverse humidity when it is being laid. All timber sold by specialist flooring companies will be supplied to the right moisture content, whether presealed or not. It is essential that, before laying, boards are left loose for a week or more to reach equilibrium with the space in which they are to be laid. In the past, before accurate moisture readings were available, floors were loosely pinned for the first year and properly cramped together and nailed down after that, but this is no longer necessary.

Once it is dry, the cellular structure of wood remains relatively porous and will absorb and give off moisture as the conditions change, causing shrinking and expansion. This must be taken into account, leaving room between the joints for wood to 'breathe'. However well-seasoned the timber may be it is likely to move after installation: tongued and grooved boards have the advantage that even if there is shrinkage, any gaps between them will be bridged by the tongue. Composite plank hardwood strip floors will be much more stable, having been prepared and stored and usually presealed to the correct moisture content.

FROM TOP *Iroko, teak, mahogany (which should only be used from properly managed sources) and American red oak.*

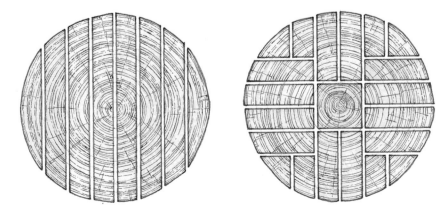

ABOVE *Cross-sections show through-sawing and quarter-sawing of timber.*

Structural Floors

There are two main types of wooden flooring: structural floors, where the boards rest over the main load-bearing joists, and overlay floors, which consist of a thinner layer of wood laid over a structural floor. Structural floors are part of the building, and in most cases you will inherit them when you move into a house or apartment. However, you may choose to replace your structural floor if you are carrying out renovation or new building work.

The long pieces of wood which make up most wooden floors are known as either boards or strips, depending on their width. Strips are less than 10cm (4in) wide, while boards are wider than this. Some hardwood flooring comes as composite boards, usually 15cm (around 6in) or wider, made up of smaller pieces, often short lengths 5cm (2in) wide, which are known as staves. Boards are generally used for structural floors, although hardwood strips can be used. Both boards and strips can also be used for overlay flooring. The structural floors of many modern houses consist of chipboard (see page 91) because it is inexpensive and builders anticipate that it will be covered.

Softwood boards are available in standard 10cm (4in), 12.5cm (5in) or 15cm (6in) widths and wider boards can be obtained. Coming as they do from trees taller and straighter than hardwood trees, softwood boards can be cut in very long lengths – up to 5m (16ft 5in). When laying new structural boards, make sure they are thick enough to span the spaces between joists without bowing. In most cases this will mean a thickness of 20 or 25mm (¾ or 1in), although you should check this with your architect, surveyor or local building inspector. The boards will generally run the length of the room across the joists, which usually span the shorter width.

If carrying out major renovations, you may need to replace rotten or very damaged floorboards. To ensure a suitable match, take a loose board from the existing floor, sand well to establish its original grain and colour, and give this to a woodyard. Replacement will seldom be exact, but this will add to the floor's character. Most structural floorboards in older houses will be made of softwoods, but it is perfectly possible to replace them with hardwood if you wish.

Wide hardwood floorboards are generally expensive, but they can look breathtaking, particularly in a large room. Bear in mind that the width of the tree determines the width of the boards, so not all timber is available in wide boards (see table on page 183). Wide boards must be cut from high-quality timber, as poor-quality boards may warp or cup. It is possible to find wide softwood boards from second-hand sources, although this is usually more expensive than using new hardwood because the salvaged timber must be reworked and prepared. However, the quality, colour, patination and overall appearance will be striking.

It is worth considering sanding existing floorboards rather than installing a new wood floor. The boards do not have to be in perfect condition, and sanding avoids the need to adjust thresholds to incorporate a change in level. Unless installing heating, most expansion and movement of the boards will have already taken place. Damaged boards can be cut out and gaps filled to produce an attractive patchwork of timber. Fill large gaps between boards with a proprietary wood-coloured epoxy resin filler or slivers of wood (see page 169). Do

ABOVE *Sanding your floor in the correct order will help minimize the sanding marks. Begin by sanding diagonally to smooth any irregularities. Only sand across the grain of the wood if the surface is still uneven after diagonal sanding; the more sanding across or diagonal to the grain, the harder it will be to finish with a smooth floor free of marks. Repeat the process rather than working the sander harder into the grain. Once the floor is smooth, sand along the grain of the wood. Finally, work along the edges of the room.*

this after a first sanding, but prior to the final sandings, and ensure the gaps are completely free of dust to help adhesion. Three or even four sandings using increasingly fine papers may be necessary on deeply marked floors. Even if you employ a specialist sanding and sealing company, this remains a very economical way of achieving a striking floor that will show off rugs and furniture to advantage. Sanding and sealing, or going further and decorating existing floors, are excellent ways of turning an old, worn floor into something special.

ABOVE *In this apartment natural floorboards can be seen at their honest best, complementing the stripped wood of the doors and windows. The boards stretching through into the next room lend a feeling of extended space to this uncluttered interior.*

Overlay Floors

Overlay flooring can be laid either over existing floorboards or on a solid concrete floor. The range of overlays available is extensive and has grown rapidly over recent years. It now includes many composite and strip systems for use on all types of structural sub-floors – wood block for use on concrete, and parquet and parquetry for use on either concrete or timber sub-floors. Some overlay systems consist of composite boards made with a thin wood veneer on a plywood or similar base, sometimes with the addition of a cork backing. These are warmer, less noisy and softer underfoot than solid boards, although the quietness can create the slightly unreal effect of walking on a 'fake' material.

Overlay systems are very suitable for existing timber suspended floors, which are usually found on the upper storeys of a house, because they are relatively light and are flexible enough to accommodate any bounce in the floor. Softwood is never used for the thinner overlay floor systems because it is not strong enough.

Both strip and board overlay floors are available in economical, presanded and prevarnished planks made up of smaller staves. These come in widths of 10, 15 or 20cm (around 4, 6 or 8in) and are usually 120 or 150cm (4 or 5ft) long. Overlay floors are available in thicknesses of 6, 9, 12 or 15mm (¼, ⅜, ½ or ⅝in) and while they are not as thin as linoleum or cork, they will add little more thickness than carpet on underlay. The long edges (and usually the short ones as well) will be tongued and grooved so that the planks interlock.

Flooring of this kind is best loosely laid over a resilient layer of foam or thin cork, and fixed together with a system of clips which fit into grooves on the backs of the planks, or are glued together effectively making a single room-sized sheet which is not normally fixed to the existing floor. However, on concrete floors and where height allows, they can be laid on timber battens which are secured to the floor below. The battens are usually 5cm (2in) wide and 15, 19 or 25mm (just over ½, ¾ or 1in) thick. One advantage of using them is that, before the boards are laid, the gaps between the battens can be filled with insulating fibre for extra warmth, as well as providing a space in which to lay electrical wiring or pipes.

These floors can be laid by an enthusiastic amateur with a little skill and patience, and some manufacturers supply them in prepacked kit form. Before you put down an overlay floor you will need to prepare the existing floor properly (see pages 169–72), and plan for the additional thickness at doors, tops of stairs, thresholds and skirtings. It is particularly important to realize that where one of the thicker overlays meets the bottom or top of stairs, it will affect the height of the first or last tread and could be a safety hazard.

Overlay systems of all kinds are usually sold with two or three coats of factory-applied protective coating, but manufacturers generally suggest applying a further one or two coats of their own sealant once the floor is laid. It is very important to use the sealer they recommend so you can be sure it is compatible with the existing finish. Apply an additional coat of sealant to increase water resistance if your floor is in a kitchen or bathroom. In areas which could get flooded, such as utility rooms or shower rooms, these floors are best avoided.

ABOVE *The strong character of this jarrah floor comes from the imaginative way in which old floorboards are re-used. Overlay panels are made up of short boards set in narrow metal frames and these are laid with the grain and direction of the wood alternating in the manner of tiles or parquet.*

ABOVE *Typical overlay floors consist of tongued and grooved boards, usually 9, 12 or 18mm (⅜, ½ or ¾in) thick, laid on a resilient mat of cork or foam over a structural floor of timber or concrete.*

OPPOSITE *These handsome random-width clear-grained polished timber boards have unusually large and definite V-shaped joints. This enables each board to be read as an individual visual element and is consistent with the overall clarity of an interior in which every surface makes a separate statement. The tatami mats set flush with the boards are joined with a similar emphasis of line.*

ABOVE *This heavily figured floor is made of strips of strongly grained light hard-wood which has been stained to give the appearance of a darker tropical wood – far better than using these endangered timbers themselves. The colours of the floor harmonize with the variety of timbers in the units.*

LEFT *This unusual floor is made of strips of wood which themselves consist of short cross-strips of different timbers. The effect is one of strongly varied colour within the discipline of the straight 'boards'.*

OPPOSITE *In a Paris apartment, these wide floor planks made of short-section staves are in a rich reddish-brown timber which forms an attractive contrast to the starkness of the glass and steel furniture.*

Parquet & Parquetry

Parquet floors usually consist of small blocks of hardwood, between 20 and 30mm (¾ and 1¼in) thick, laid out in various geometric patterns and designs. Traditionally the blocks were laid like bricks in a herringbone pattern following the direction of travel across the room, with a straight border of blocks around the perimeter of the walls. However, shaped blocks can also be used to create basketweave or more complex patterns (see pages 12–13). They used to be set in hot mastic or bitumen, but contemporary PVA and similar adhesives are more practical and wood-coloured. Contact adhesives are not recommended, as the pieces need to be pushed firmly against each other. Laying an original parquet floor requires considerable skill and craftsmanship and will generally be expensive. However, some specialist companies manufacture prefabricated panels, 30cm (12in) or 45cm (18in) square, each one comprising several blocks. These are generally 6–14mm (¼–½in) thick, much thinner than traditional individual blocks, and come in a variety of timbers. To reduce the expense you can use larger blocks and thus create patterns on a broader scale, or confine the area of parquet to a central field and fill the perimeter of the room, together with any alcoves and bays, with plain strip or plank timber.

It is also possible to buy reclaimed woodblock floors, although these have their own associated problems. You will need to ensure that all traces of the original adhesive are completely removed, and that the adhesive you plan to use is compatible with the existing floor surface. Remember also that reclaimed parquet blocks will have worn, so it may be difficult to match pieces without wastage. Minor differences can probably be evened out by sanding; as for any reclaimed wood, this is normally done after the entire floor has been laid.

An elaboration of the traditional parquet floor, parquetry is essentially a large-scale version of marquetry, where individual pieces of wood are shaped and laid in elaborate patterns by highly skilled craftsmen. Today, as with parquet, parquetry is most affordable when bought as prefabricated units in a range of patterns. If you are planning a parquetry floor it is important to make sure that the design complements the layout of the room and that any borders of the pattern echo its shape. The rich, elaborate patterns of parquetry can be somewhat overpowering and sombre, and are best suited to large, formal rooms or to hallways, where their beauty can be fully appreciated. Recent developments in laser cutting techniques have radically reduced the cost of parquet floors.

BELOW *Many designs are possible with custom-made parquetry. In the centrepiece, the craftsman has arranged the grain of the timber so that it radiates with the star pattern.*

OPPOSITE *In this exquisite parquet floor, the delicate geometry of the design and the light tone of the bleached wood complement the solid natural feel created by the strong grain and exposed fixings.*

RIGHT *Here the strongly figured grain of the oak boards contrasts with the unfigured flat colour of the border. Dark border lines like these are often made of ebony, but the same effect could be achieved by staining.*

Plywood & Chipboard

Some of the most stylish and economical floors can be created by the use of composite boards such as plywood and chipboard, which are made from various kinds of softwood. Plywood consists of three or more thin sheets of wood glued together under pressure, with the grain of one layer at right angles to the grain of the adjoining layer. Its relative strength and stability makes it ideal for use on floors. Plywoods are available with a surface veneer of many different types of timber, and can be between 4 and 18mm (just over ⅛ and ¾in) thick depending on the number of layers in their composition. They come in standard sheet sizes of 1.2×2.4m (4×8ft) or 1.5×3m (5×10ft), although these can be cut into any shape. You might, for example, consider making 60cm (2ft) squares and laying them with the grains in alternating directions to create a crisp subtle chequerboard pattern.

Chipboard is manufactured from small chips of softwood bound together with glue or resin under heat and pressure. Specialist flooring grade chipboard is available, which is denser and has a smoother finish than ordinary chipboard. Many new houses have structural floors constructed from chipboard sheets. These come in a variety of sizes, the most common of which are 0.6×2.4m (2×8ft), 1.2×2.4m (4×8ft) and 1.2m (4ft) square. Chipboard degrades quickly when moist, so it is best to use the water-resistant variety in bathrooms and kitchens. It makes a good economical base for painting and takes colour well.

One particularly hard-wearing and inexpensive type of thin overlay is hardboard (also known as Masonite). Like chipboard, this is made by binding compressed sawdust and wood chips together with resin or adhesive. It is sold with either a normal finish or tempered with oil to make it water-resistant. Available in 4mm (just over ⅛in) and 6mm (¼in) thicknesses, it has an attractive rich brown colour, does not show dirt stains and polishes well to a high gloss. It can also be painted or stencilled to create patterns.

Plywood and hardboard can be laid over existing floors and are frequently used to cover damaged wooden boards to provide an even surface on which to lay sheet materials, ceramics or carpet. Overlays of this type should usually be no thicker than 6mm (¼in) so they are flexible enough to follow the lie of the sub-floor to which they are pinned. Since even the thinnest chipboard is around 12mm (½in) thick, it is not suitable for overlaying.

There has been some environmental concern about composite wood- and fibre-based boards because most have until recently been made using formaldehyde glues and other toxic substances. However, formaldehyde-free chipboard is now available from some suppliers.

To achieve a unified appearance at relatively low cost, plywood can be used, as in this kitchen, both as a covering for the floor and to face fitted cupboards and work units. The large squares of even-grained veneer are clear, simple elements in a design where each component in the room has a part to play in building up the overall composition. This flat, pale, undemonstrative floor makes a plain, warm background to the crisp, practical metal furniture.

Bleaching, Liming & Staining

Wooden floorboards can be lightened by bleaching or liming. Proprietary woodbleach will make the wood almost white and is useful if you are planning to stain bare untreated boards, since the natural colour inherent in the wood may otherwise distort the stain tone. However, you should use bleach with care if you wish to retain some of the natural colouring.

The technique of liming was originally developed for open-grained hardwoods, such as oak, but is now considered suitable for other timbers. Start by brushing the wood with a coarse wire brush along the grain. Then brush or rub on a white pigment. For softwoods and beech, it is best to brush on thin white paint; for less absorbent woods you can choose between paint, distemper, filler or liming wax. When dry, wax-limed boards can simply be polished, while wood limed with other pigments should be be sealed with varnish or wax.

Stains are applied directly to the bare wood. Since they act as a tint rather than a covering, they leave the grain attractively visible and slightly darker. They are obtainable in a range of shades which imitate the colours of natural timbers, as well as in bright or muted primary colours. Oil-based stains tend to give the most even results, while water-based products are somewhat thin and require several coats. Spirit stains penetrate well, but they dry very quickly and therefore need to be applied over smaller areas, which can make even application difficult. If you decide to apply woodstain, it is particularly important to start with a smooth surface, since rougher areas will absorb more stain and appear darker. You may therefore need to sand the wood extremely carefully. A very attractive parquetry effect can be created by colouring a geometric pattern, such as squares or diamonds, with stains that imitate different timbers: reddy brown mahogany with light oak or pine, for example. To make the finished effect more realistic and to keep the edges neat, score joint lines into the surface with a sharp knife. Stained floors can be either waxed or varnished to seal them, providing that the sealer is compatible with the stain.

Painting

Painting offers more scope for the imaginative use of colour and pattern than any other technique. A common practice in past centuries, particularly to imitate stone and to decorate plain wooden boards, the use of paint on floors has recently undergone a revival with the growth in do-it-yourself home decorating. Paint can be applied to softwood, chipboard and hardboard, as well as to sand and cement screed. A variety of techniques can be employed, including stencilling and dragging, antiquing and marbling. On wooden floors you may wish to try combining a stained base with painted decoration. Paints and stains can be considerably more economical than many other kinds of floor covering, even when applied by a professional decorator, and need not necessarily be extended to the whole area of a room. You might, for example, aim for a traditional effect by painting a bare floor surrounding an area of carpet.

Paint gives the opportunity to achieve a range of finishes, from transparent pale-coloured washes, which reveal the grain, to plain opaque colours, which

ABOVE *This grey-stained floor of narrow boards works together with the natural wide boarding of the wall to create a simple richness typical of Scandinavian design. The stain has been applied sparingly to the floor so that the warm tone and grain of the wood show through.*

OPPOSITE *The strength and character of this eighteenth-century oak parquet floor derive from the bold and simple geometry of the pieces. The pattern is emphasized by the open joints. To recreate this look, it is possible to use reclaimed timber. Since old boards are often damaged, cutting them into short lengths is an excellent way to salvage them.*

ABOVE *Investment in good modern furniture does not require an equally expensive floor treatment. The simple old painted boards act as a positive contrast, their rough character highlighting the precision of the furniture. The yellow timber of the table legs and the blue-grey of the floor are echoed in the colour scheme of the walls to create a harmonious whole.*

more or less conceal it. Opaque painted surfaces can be ornamented with simple repeat patterns or elaborate large-scale designs. The general design principles for floors discussed on pages 11–24 apply equally when designing with paint. In rooms with little furniture, for example, or those where the use is specific and unchanging, such as bathrooms or entrance halls, a bold pattern may be attractive. Generally, however, you should avoid creating a floor so striking and insistent that it dominates other elements in the room. In most cases, paint works best as a plain background for rugs or when applied in simple repeat patterns, such as chequerboards or large squares with inset key squares, either over a whole room or as borders.

Although paint will conceal all sorts of blemishes, proper preparation is always worthwhile to ensure a long-lasting finish. Begin by repairing any major cracks and nailing or screwing down loose boards (see page 169–170). Remove all traces of old varnish and polish by applying wood stripper and scrubbing with methylated spirit. Then sand the floor, either by hand over small areas or with a power sander over the entire surface. There is no need to remove all previous paint providing it is firm, although existing dark colours may be difficult to cover with paler shades.

Where the existing floor is in a bad condition, you could consider covering it completely, either by overlaying the entire surface with hardboard, which can then be painted, or by painting pieces of hardboard to be laid in sections, as you would parquet. The joints in sectioned hardboard can be incorporated into the final design so that they are less evident. Squares of 60×60cm (2×2ft), for example, are easy to handle and can be painted in two different colours to make an inexpensive chequerboard pattern.

For plain painted backgrounds start by applying a wood primer, followed by two coats of undercoat. Match the tone of the undercoat to the final colour, but avoid using precisely the same shade so that any patches that have been missed with the topcoat are immediately apparent. Plan your painting so that you work outwards towards the door. Since the whole surface will eventually be given a protective varnish there is no need to use gloss paint for the final coat of colour. Flat oils or even vinyl matt paints are much easier to apply. Design motifs or patterns should ideally be painted in flat oils or eggshell. It may be helpful to outline the pattern first with a small brush and then fill in larger areas with a wide one. Stencils are useful for repeat patterns but only work well on relatively smooth floors, although stencilled patterns on squares of hardboard laid as tiles offer exciting opportunities for colourful designs. You can be more adventurous and use paint techniques such as wood-graining or marbling to develop sophisticated patterns and designs.

Once dry, a painted floor should be covered with a minimum of three coats of a compatible protective varnish, or five coats in areas of heavy traffic.

OPPOSITE *In an early nineteenth-century house in West Virginia, this floor is painted in tones of blue to create a strong geometric form which emphasizes the centrality of the round table, while allowing the lines of the boards to run through the pattern. Confining the colours within a similar tonal value ensures that the large bold pattern, with its rigid symmetry, does not completely dominate the room.*

PAINTING

OPPOSITE *The painted wood, simple design and restrained use of detail in this entrance hall are typical of Swedish decorative schemes. Faded blue and yellow colours on the floor complement the understated tones of the walls, furniture and woodwork. A chequerboard pattern has been created by colourwashing: thick paint would obliterate the texture of the wood, but brushing on one or two coats of very dilute emulsion (latex) allows the paint to act like a stain, letting the natural grain of the wood show through.*

BELOW *This trompe-l'oeil pattern painted on a timber floor evokes a series of tumbling boxes seen in perspective. First developed by Roman mosaic artists and revived and used extensively by American patchwork-quilt makers in the nineteenth century, the illusion depends for its success on the subtlety of colours used to suggest shadow and light on the sides of the boxes. Outlines were first brushed in with cerulean blue, then the blocks were painstakingly colourwashed in earth tones.*

97

Sealing & Protecting

All wood floors that are not prefinished must be sealed against dirt, discoloration and moisture. Clear sealants can be applied to bare sanded wood or to wood which has been painted or stained, or the sealant itself can be tinted to add colour to the floor. There are three main types of sealant: waxes, oils and varnishes. All are applied after the floor has been laid.

Although the least practical, wax is the most beautiful of these options: nothing can imitate the soft warm lustre of a well-maintained waxed floor. Traditionally, a beeswax and turpentine mixture was used, but this is not resistant to water, alcohol or everyday wear. Today it is possible to obtain hardwearing natural waxes specially formulated for floors and usually derived from the leaves of the Brazilian carnauba palm. There are also a number of excellent synthetic waxes which are by-products of the petrochemical industry. You will need to reapply a wax finish about three times a year over the entire floor, and any damage can easily be repaired by adding extra layers of wax and buffing regularly. In order to prevent successive coats of wax soaking into the wood, apply a very thin coat of polyurethane varnish or button polish and allow to dry before applying the wax thinly with a soft cloth.

BELOW *Highly polished to protect it from scuffs and other damage, the elaborate graining patterns of this overlay parquet floor are an appropriate match for the high-quality joinery of this dressing room.*

Oil has the benefit of being naturally water-resistant and easily applied. You will need to apply three to four coats of oil to seal bare wood completely, with perhaps a further coat of wax to protect the finished surface against wear. Tung oil, derived from the seeds of the Chinese tung tree, is extremely resistant to heat, water and alcohol and is the main constituent of many oil-based floor sealants. Used on its own, it will take about four days to dry between coats. Danish oil, a mixture of tung oil and various driers and other agents, will dry within two to four hours and is particularly hard-wearing. Teak oil is also produced from tung oil, but with the addition of boiled linseed oil which gives the finished floor a darker colour.

Varnishes were originally made from boiled linseed oil and natural resins. Although tough and hard-wearing, traditional varnishes took about three days to dry, during which time dust and dirt could ruin the tacky surface. These have now largely been superseded by quick-drying urethane compounds produced by the petrochemical industry, which are still generally known as varnishes.

Early polyurethane varnishes were inflexible and unable to respond to movement in the wood, which resulted in crazing and cracking. However, modern water-based acrylic urethane co-polymers are flexible, colourless and resistant to heat, dirt and water, making them ideal for any location. In general three coats should be enough to protect the wood against normal use, with an extra coat in kitchens and bathrooms. Gloss or semi-gloss polyurethane varnish forms the toughest surface, while matt versions are less durable.

Polyurethane is much easier to apply when thinned, but each progressive layer should be less dilute. To ensure a good finish, allow each coat to dry completely, and then sand lightly before adding the next one. For an extremely long-lasting seal, two-pack varnishes, which need to be used within a few hours of mixing, are also available. When applying any kind of varnish, it is essential to wear a mask and to ensure that the room is well ventilated and dust-free. Polyurethaned floors are very easy to clean using a damp cloth or mop, but once the surface has broken down there is no alternative but to sand the entire floor and apply a new coat.

A very high-gloss and resistant form of varnish, lacquer is tougher than polyurethane although considerably more expensive. A lacquered finish is created by building up successive layers of translucent glaze, which can be tinted in a wide variety of colours. One benefit of lacquer, apart from its beautiful glossy sheen, is that it settles into a smooth coat without brush marks when dry.

If you have chosen presanded and varnished wood flooring systems, you will usually need to apply a single coat of the manufacturer's finish after laying but will not have to reseal the floor for many years. Whatever sealant you use, you should always try your intended treatment on a small area or a sample of the same timber and wait till the treatment is dry, including trials with the type of polish you anticipate using in the future. Most reputable manufacturers will have a range of colours, varnishes and stains suitable for their products. Avoid using products that are more than a year old.

BELOW *Provided it is well sealed, there is no reason why wood cannot be used even in wet areas. Here wide boards of heavily figured timber create a grandeur, emphasized by the generosity of space round the large freestanding washbasin.*

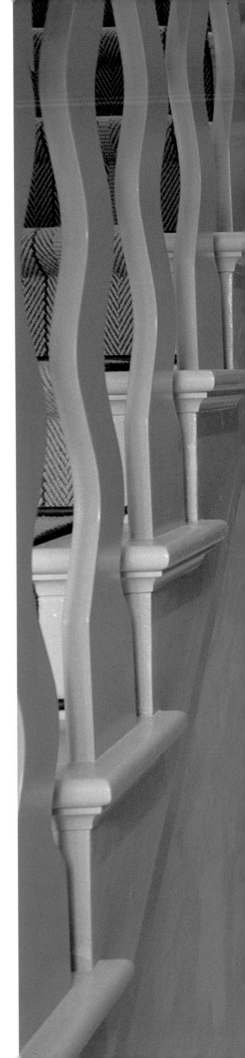

There is a moment of immense satisfaction when a carpet or rug goes down. The noise of construction has stopped, the dust has gone and the paint is dry. The time has come to start living in your space. The magic of carpet works on all the senses – the spaces become quiet and warm and your eyes are drawn across the whole floor. If the colour you have chosen harmonizes with the wall, the decorations and carpet will create a complete and satisfying environment.

The terms 'carpet' and 'rug' are used here not to define their form of construction but to distinguish size and use. 'Carpet' denotes a large floor covering that can be cut to suit any room, while 'rug' means a loose-laid piece of a size and design determined by the maker. The history and origins of both types can be traced as one, since the techniques for mechanized weaving of carpet on the roll are those developed by early rug weavers. Before deciding whether to have fitted carpets or a scattering of rugs, you should think carefully about the style of your furniture and the nature of your floors. As an overall multifunctional covering, fitted carpet offers many advantages and is, by and large, good value for money. It hides poor-quality structural floors; when combined with underlay, it gives a feeling of softness and luxury and provides good sound insulation; it acts as an excellent draught proofer over ill-fitting boards on a ground floor; and tests have shown that fitting carpet can reduce heating consumption by as much as 8.5–12.5%. A plain carpet also creates a single unifying background throughout a house or apartment and makes a small space feel larger.

Rugs can be just as successful in suggesting softness and luxury, whether you buy oriental antiques, modern crafted pieces or mass-produced rag rugs and dhurries. They bring warmth to hard floors and will brighten a plain fitted carpet. Generally available in a wide range of colours, patterns and shapes, and at prices to suit every pocket, rugs allow you to express your individuality and give you the flexibility to change your furnishing schemes without replacing the entire carpet. The simplest hearthrug will emphasize the fireplace as a focal point, while a runner viewed through an open doorway creates a link with the space beyond and a bright rug will lighten a dark corner. Unlike fitted carpet, rugs are easy to move from house to house and, in the case of antiques, can be exchanged through specialist dealers.

Rugs and carpets have been used to cover floors in virtually every part of the world since records began. As early as the eighth century BC, rugs were depicted

A red kelim laid as a runner makes a glowing invitation to this hall. The runner beyond heightens the sense of a progression *through the series of doorways. The grey-green paint of skirting and architrave complements the warm tones in the kelim.*

100

ABOVE *A wide variety of thick woollen rugs are woven to designs by modern artists and can be used as a centrepiece in any room. This striking design is by the Swiss painter Paul Klee.*

OPPOSITE *This sculptural interior, with its white ceiling, doors and walls, requires something to soften the hard floor. The patterns of the dark blue and white kelim are appropriately bold and geometric for the setting and display the characteristic stepped edges of the colour blocks found in flatweave rugs.*

in Assyrian carvings; and the oldest surviving carpet is a woollen felt square embroidered with feline heads, found in Southern Russia and dated 2500 BC. Although production of patterned rugs with knotted piles or embroidered motifs was well established in many parts of Asia by the second century AD, it was not until the Middle Ages that rugs from these areas were seen in Europe in any numbers. By the fifteenth century, so-called 'Turkye' carpets were adorning many interiors and demand from European customers spurred the growth of systematized workshops in Persia, the Caucasus and Egypt.

During the next two to three hundred years, carpet manufacture was also developed in Belgium, France and Poland. The English industry started in the eighteenth century, when Huguenot weavers organized production in London, Axminster, Wilton and Kidderminster, where there were plentiful supplies of good-quality wool and clean water for the washing and dyeing of yarns. An important technological breakthrough occurred in 1745, when the French textile manufacturer Jacquard introduced a system of automated colour selection using punched cards. This facilitated production of complex repeat patterns and allowed carpets to be made to measure for large aristocratic homes. At first the designs were Far Eastern in inspiration, but soon a more European style developed, with motifs and borders based on classical ornament.

Mechanized looms were developed in Boston in 1841. These revolutionized carpet production and were soon in use elsewhere, particularly in Europe and Canada. While emulating the construction and design of hand-made carpets in most respects, mass-produced carpets were cheaper and more widely affordable. When Western manufacture expanded during the nineteenth century, the production of hand-made rugs in the East at first declined, but it later revived as Western interest in Eastern art grew and as the Arts and Crafts movement fostered a new emphasis on traditional weaving.

As European and American craftsmen began to see rugs as a suitable medium for their skills, pioneering designers at the Bauhaus and others such as Eileen Gray, Frank Lloyd-Wright and Marion Dorn created boldly coloured floor coverings in a modern idiom. Concurrently a fascination in America with Navaho weaving grew, for the most part in Mexico, into an industry making rugs based on these bold abstract designs. In the East, factories were set up in Pakistan, Turkey and India to produce mechanically woven rugs with traditional designs. Colourful and economic rugs from all over the world, together with the high-quality work of artist-craftsmen, provide a wealth of choice today.

Since the 1950s, when newly developed synthetic yarns and tufted manufacturing techniques made mass-produced carpet cheaper, the twentieth-century British and American dream of wall-to-wall floor covering throughout the house has been largely met. While fitted carpets offer the only comfortable and practical way of bringing warmth to cold, draughty floors, improved construction and insulation now mean hard floors do not have some of these problems. The current fashion for rugs of all sorts has been created partly by the European design tradition which lays emphasis on the beauty of plain floors of timber, stone or tiles covered with rugs for both decoration and softness.

Traditionally both rugs and carpets were made using either pile or flatweave construction. These two basic methods still form the basis of most craft weaving today, and it is from them that mass-production techniques were developed.

Flatweave Rugs & Carpets

Otherwise known as tapestry or kelim weaving, the technique of flatweaving is almost universal and is found from the Americas, through Europe and North Africa to India. Two basic threads are used in flatweaving, the warp and the weft. The weft creates the wearing surface and the design. Colour changes are achieved by weaving in stripes or in separate adjacent blocks of different shades, leaving characteristic small gaps between different blocks of colour, which are sometimes sewn together. To avoid the gaps becoming too wide, the patterns are often stepped sideways. The flatweaving process lends itself more successfully to mechanization than knotting, and machine-made kelims and flatwoven rugs are produced throughout the world, particularly in Mexico, Portugal, Morocco, Turkey, Pakistan and India, in a great range of sizes and colours.

Kelims come from some of the same geographical regions as knotted oriental rugs – particularly Asia Minor – and are made with the same natural dyes, wools and regional patterns, but are formed using the more basic and less luxurious flatweave technique, hence the term 'kelim weave'. These sturdy rugs (sometimes used as animal covers and saddle bags) have become ever more popular as they have stepped changes of colour (derived from the weaving technique) and a strong modern character. Figures and floral patterns are stylized, and patterns are geometric and bold.

Dhurries are flatwoven cotton rugs which were originally made in India for use as underlays beneath more precious carpets, but developed into economic and colourful rugs incorporating motifs from other weaving cultures, in particular Persian and Caucasian or Turkish geometric patterns. They are available in many sizes, the most popular being approximately 120×80cm (48×30in); 180×100cm (6ft×3ft 3in) and 240×150cm (8×5ft). While less thick and sumptuous than kelims, dhurries are easier to wash and are ideal for hallways and playrooms.

Embroidered and crocheted rugs come in many patterns and designs. Depending on the materials used, they can be reasonably hard-wearing, but being generally thinner are more commonly used as wall hangings or drapes.

Braided rugs are made from long strips of plaited braids laced together, often in circles or ovals. They can be made with new yarn or strips of used fabrics, and the build-up of layers creates a thick heavy texture. The overall effect is usually one of peppered colour.

Rag rugs have been woven by peasants in many countries as a way to recycle fabric. Flatwoven rag rugs are constructed from threads of warp interwoven with a weft of fabric strip. Rags may also be attached to a backing to form pile rugs. Mass-produced rag rugs are made in various places, particularly Portugal, Greece and Scandinavia, and provide economic practical decoration on hard floors.

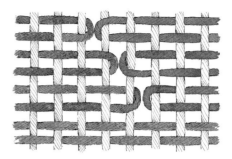

ABOVE *Flatweave or kelim weaving, showing the joint between the blocks of colour, which produces tiny slits in the surface and the characteristic stepped pattern.*

OPPOSITE *This flatweave Scandinavian rag rug has a subtlety similar to the tiles in a traditional stove. The simple repeated pattern, widely spaced in a plain, textured background, produces a restful rhythm.*

RIGHT ABOVE *The stepped geometry typical of kelim weave is evident in an antique rug.*

RIGHT BELOW *A contemporary flatweave design derives its beauty partly from the subtle variety of tones in batch-dyed wools.*

Pile Rugs & Carpets

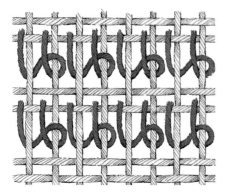

Knotted pile rugs and carpets are found in all parts of the world; hand-made knotted rugs from the Middle East are perhaps the finest. Three types of thread are involved in the construction of knotted pile rugs: the warp, the weft and the pile. First the warp threads are tied lengthwise across a frame. Short lengths of yarn forming the pile are then knotted in rows round the warp threads and held in place by a weft thread woven from side to side. After weaving, the pile threads are trimmed to an even length. The quality of the rug will depend to a large extent on the density of pile. This is normally expressed in terms of knots per square centimetre of surface area and ranges from 4–8 knots for the coarsest rugs to 36–50 for very fine examples. For mass-produced carpet, quality is expressed in terms of weight of pile.

Hand-knotted rugs were originally made with traditional patterns which were memorized and seldom repeated exactly, which gives the more primitive examples their charming irregularity. As workshops developed, the designs were recorded on squared paper and kept in front of the weaver or, for larger rugs, they were called by an experienced weaver who sang the changes to the people working at the loom. The size of a hand-made rug is determined by the size of the loom, which for nomadic weavers had of necessity to be small. Maximum widths for nomadic rugs tend to be around 120cm (4ft), while carpets up to 300 and 350cm (10 and 12ft) were produced in the great Persian weaving centres and in Cairo. Knotted rugs are today mass-produced in Pakistan, India, Turkey, Iran, Morocco and Spain. Technically of a high standard, with dense pile, these modern works lack the subtle variations and colourings of traditional examples.

Oriental rugs are a highly specialized subject, about which much has been written. If you are considering these, it pays to study the books and always to buy from one of the many specialist and reputable dealers who have a wide stock of different types of rugs and may also carry out repairs. Avoid buying at auction unless you have some knowledge.

Other forms of pile rugs are made by adding the pile to a prewoven backing, either by hooking loops of wool, cotton or tweed yarns into it or by inserting tufts of yarn with needles. Hooked rugs were probably first produced by the Vikings, but some of the most attractive were made by American pioneers and they are common to many folk cultures. Rag rugs can also be made in this way.

ABOVE *The face of a pile rug is made from short threads knotted over the long warp threads and held in place by the weft, which is beaten down onto each row of knots. The upper diagram shows a symmetrical Turkish or Ghiordes knot, the lower the Persian or Senneh knot. Strictly speaking these are not knots at all, but loops.*

RIGHT *Antiques, such as this hand-knotted pile rug, derive their beautiful tones from the use of vegetable dyes and mineral extracts. As nomadic and rural peoples developed the skills to create a range of colours from the plants around them, each weaving region acquired a distinctive palette based on what was available in the area. Blacks, for example, have been made in different parts of the world from oak gall, iron, tea or walnut bark; reds from* rhubarb, lichens or the cochineal insect. *To keep the colour fast, the dissolved dye substances require the addition of a mordant, such as salt, slaked lime, vinegar or even urine – which explains why some Eastern rugs will smell when washed. While the early twentieth-century aniline dyes used in the East have proved unsatisfactory, leading to colour runs and fading, better-quality chemical dyes have since become widely available.*

Mechanically Produced Carpet

The three most widely available types of machine-made carpet are woven, tufted and bonded. Woven carpet can be divided into two main kinds: Axminster and Wilton, both of which are extremely durable. Broadly speaking, Axminster carpet is formed in the same way as knotted rugs, with short pile threads being woven into a warp and weft structure. Like traditional rugs, Axminster can theoretically use an infinite number of colours for each strand of pile, but in practice 'spool' Axminster uses between eight and twelve colours. The development of computer-controlled looms has allowed some companies to offer bespoke designs. The minimum order for these is usually 80 square metres (95 square yards) – about the size of a small house. While Axminster is characterized by design versatility, the distinguishing feature of Wilton is its thickness. This is produced by weaving the pile threads into the backing and then pulling them through in the form of loops, which may be cut to create a velvet effect. Colour combinations are limited by the use of about eight different yarns.

Tufted carpet, developed as a more economical form, is made by inserting tufts of pile yarn with needles into a prewoven backing, on the same principle as a hooked rug. Generally the backing consists of jute, which is then covered with a latex coating to anchor the tufts in place and finally given a secondary hessian backing. Tufted carpet is available in a wide variety of colours but a more limited range of patterns. It often contains a high proportion of artificial fibres and was once thought much inferior to woven carpet, although better-quality yarns and backings have improved appearance and wear considerably.

Research and use have demonstrated that carpet with a pile blend of 80% wool to 20% nylon offers the optimum balance between comfort, colour retention and wear. The carpet trade has coined the useful term 'uglying out' to describe a decline in appearance, as opposed to wearing out. Carpets with a higher proportion of man-made fibres are cheaper but tend to ugly out more quickly than wool carpets, although in areas likely to be subject to rough use or to water spills carpets made entirely of synthetic fibres are a good choice.

Fibre-bonded or needlepunch carpets consist of a sandwich of felt-like fabrics bonded on either side of a prewoven core by many very fine threads of artificial fibre. They are more like felts than woven carpets and are usually made with a high proportion of polypropylene and other synthetic fibres. They tend to be plain but it is possible to find a limited range with printed patterns. Less soft underfoot than pile, needlepunch and bonded carpets are resistant to wear and liquid and are therefore generally used in service areas.

Carpet tiles are available in woven, tufted and bonded types, and in many combinations of wool and synthetic fibres, although they are occasionally made in the highest grade 80/20 wool/nylon blend. They are not laid on underlay but have sufficiently thick backings to allow them to hug the floor and do not need

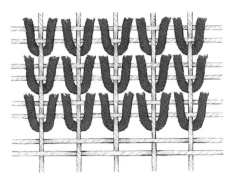

ABOVE *In mechanically produced Axminster carpet the loops are held in place by the weft in a similar way to knotted pile rugs. When cut, the loops give a velvet effect. Left uncut in a twist effect, they have greater resilience.*

BELOW *Carpet tiles are now very versatile and can be cut to create interesting and original combinations of colour and pattern. They are particularly useful in areas which suffer heavy wear, where they can be lifted and replaced as required.*

CLOCKWISE FROM TOP LEFT *Axminster showing its versatility in creating borders and patterns; tufted wool loop pile in natural shades with a heavy rib texture; a bold multicoloured Axminster; Berber* *overall natural carpet with small jewel-like geometric motifs; the strong texture characteristic of twisted Wilton; a simple overall design in 80/20 wool/nylon which will retain its appearance for a long time.*

to be stuck down with tape for domestic use except in areas where there is directional movement, at the tops and bottoms of flights of stairs or for access flooring in offices, for example. Carpet tiles come in plain or variegated colours and in dimensions of 50×50cm (20×20in). When laying, it is important to ensure that they are tightly butted together and that cut perimeter tiles fit closely against the skirting.

Haircord carpet is usually composed of 80% animal hair and 20% nylon and other artificial fibres; it has now been largely replaced by synthetic cord carpet. It is made as a continuous corrugated fabric bonded to a hessian backing, which gives it its characteristic ribbed effect. Produced in a range of plain bright colours, it is tough, inexpensive and suitable for contract use. It is relatively thin, and it is recommended that it is stuck down directly on the floor without underlay. Cord carpet is never very soft underfoot.

Berber carpet is not, as is commonly assumed, the name of a construction method, but refers to the overall natural flecked appearance of the pile created by the mixture of dyed and undyed wools, usually beige or oatmeal in colour. Berber carpets can be woven or tufted.

OPPOSITE *The designer of this Majorcan farmhouse bedroom, Mimi O'Connell, opted for the simplicity of white on white, with accents of antique gold and iron. A Sardinian carpet, specially commissioned for the room, is pivotal to its decorative scheme. The repeating central flower-and-leaf motif framed in scalloped lozenges is a modern version of the traditional cloud medallion used in Turkish and Caucasian flatweave rugs, although this carpet has a cut and carved pile.*

LEFT *The designer has emphasized the sculptural quality of the flat planes in these spaces, and this strong plain floor creates a powerful horizontal element in the composition, quite different from the more usual use of a plain carpet as a neutral background. Without any soft furnishings the carpet is of crucial importance in providing comfort.*

Yarns & Fibres

Since the quality of carpets and rugs depends partly on the nature of the yarns used to make them, it is worth considering the attributes of the different fibres available before you make your final choice. At one time all carpets and rugs were made of natural fibres spun into usable lengths. Some, such as cotton and linen, were of vegetable origin; others were made of the hair of animals such as goats, sheep, alpaca and so on. Developments in the petrochemical industry in the 1950s enabled manufacturers to produce synthetic fibres, which were extruded from chemical compounds and were more economic. Carpets made from artificial fibres remain, for the most part, less expensive than those woven from natural ones.

Wool has been the foundation for almost every sort of rug and carpet over many centuries, particularly in parts of the world with colder climates where sheep are bred. Its essential advantage lies in its unique combination of strength, suppleness, warmth and low absorbency. It sheds water, resists staining, is a good insulator and takes dyes well. Because it is so resilient, it recovers better than any other fibre from foot and furniture pressure and will continue to look good for longer. Indeed a good-quality 80/20 wool/nylon carpet should retain a reasonable appearance for much longer than the manufacturers' claims of at least seven to ten years. Wool does not support combustion, while synthetic fibres do and some give off toxic fumes. Many traditional rugs combine a wool pile with cotton warp and weft for economy and availability. Today the backings of commercially produced carpet tend to be made of jute or polypropylene.

Cotton has traditionally been grown in the warmer climates of Egypt and India, and these countries have long produced exceptionally fine cotton rugs. Although it tends to shrink when wet, cotton combines lightness and pliability with considerable strength for its thickness and is occasionally blended with other fibres to make carpet.

Silk shares properties of both vegetable and animal fibres. It is considerably more absorbent than other natural fibres and takes dye well, producing brilliantly coloured, soft-textured rugs.

Nylon is very tough, is resistant to abrasion and does not absorb moisture. It is consequently used in carpets designed for wet areas. Although it has a high propensity to soil, it can be specially treated to make it stain-resistant. Nylon, like the other synthetic fibres mentioned below, is sold under a variety of brand names and is often combined with wool in different proportions. As a general rule, a mix of 80% wool to 20% nylon has proven to be the best for wear and appearance retention.

Polyester is a strong fibre, which resists wear, does not stretch and is frequently blended with wools to provide increased strength. It is also used in combination with other synthetic materials, such as nylon.

Acrylic is soft and supple, and cheap to produce. It is sometimes blended with more expensive fine wools or hairs, although, like lambswool, it has a tendency to 'pill'.

Polypropylene is hard-wearing and easy to clean. However, carpet made entirely of this material will feel somewhat rough and appear shiny.

This room is governed by clean strong lines which emphasize the basic architectural shapes. The carpet design, with its undemonstrative grid of lines forms a subtle linear pattern on a background similar in tone to the walls.

Contemporary designer rugs can be as thick and luxurious as traditional pile rugs or carpet. Produced in designs ranging from bold and geometrical to simple and plain, they can look good in traditional or contemporary rooms and sit no less comfortably with antiques than with modern furniture. Craftsman-produced rugs, like oriental pieces, will give a unique and personal character to a room.

Selecting a Carpet or Rug

Manufacturers use an eight-point grading system which categorizes carpet into four domestic and four contract grades: light duty, medium duty, heavy duty and extra heavy for each group. Most makes which carry the independent assessment of the International Wool Secretariat or Woolmark accreditation will be labelled accordingly, although this system of categorization is under review. Various tests are used to determine the grade given to any particular carpet. These include appearance retention, which is expressed on a scale of 1–5, pile weight and colourfastness. Computerized loom technology has enabled manufacturers to create all manner of innovations, among them 'high low' carpets with sculpted pile. These are difficult to test. But the general rule seems to be that patterned carpets of darker colours and heavier grades will continue to look good for longer than plainer or lighter grade carpets in paler shades.

Commercial carpets use synthetic dyes and are graded according to colourfastness. A scale of 1–8 is used, although above 6 is the highest practical grade for black. For darker colours 5 is a good-quality standard and for pastel shades 4 is acceptable. Standards of 3 or less should be avoided. The degree to which carpet will fade is affected by its exposure to light and sun and tends to be more pronounced with pastel colours.

You will also find carpets that have been treated to resist soiling and staining, while carpets made specifically for laying in wet areas will be marked as such. Only you can decide where and how your carpet is to be used, but the following points may be helpful.

Bedrooms can be carpeted with light domestic grade and velvet pile types, although thicker pile Wilton is probably the most luxurious. You may also wish to surround the bed with rugs. Indeed, in the eighteenth century, long strips of rug were formed into U-shapes specifically for this purpose.

Bathrooms tend to be austere and carpet will help to bring a sense of warmth to the floor, but you should avoid any kinds that are liable to be affected by damp. Medium domestic grade is suitable, and there is no need to assume that the carpet must be made of synthetic fibres since woven woollen types are perfectly practical. Cotton dhurries are also excellent in bathrooms.

Kitchens and utility rooms are better fitted with tiled, wooden or other floors which are easy to clean. Although some bonded and needlepunch carpets are specially formulated for kitchen use, the high proportion of artificial fibres in their construction makes them somewhat harsh. The danger of tripping suggests that rugs should be avoided.

Dining rooms require medium- or heavy-duty domestic grades of carpet. Fitted carpet will not be scuffed or lifted by chairs, as rugs tend to be. If you do wish to place a rug under the table, cup the feet of the table and rotate the rug at intervals to change the pattern of wear.

Living rooms are ideally suited to both carpets and rugs and, as for dining rooms, you should choose from the medium- and heavy-duty domestic grades. If using rugs, take note of the pattern of heaviest use in the room and put the most precious rugs in the more out-of-the-way corners.

Hallways are subjected to more wear and dirt than any other area of the home and benefit from heavy- or extra-heavy duty grades of carpet. Protect

ABOVE *This fitted twist carpet has enough texture to contrast with flat walls and polished wood, yet its neutral tone blends with the wallpaper to form a background for the antique bed, the pedestal table and the fireplace, which are the main features of the room.*

OPPOSITE *In contrast to the demure effect of a plain carpet above, this brightly checked fitted carpet dominates the spaces. Its tartan lines lead the eye across the room and up the stairs, and are complemented by an equally bold treatment of walls, paintwork and furnishings.*

carpets and rugs by making sure you have the largest possible doormat. The general view is that after you have entered a room from outside most dirt stays on your shoes for the first eight paces. If your budget will not stretch to good-quality woven 80/20 wool/nylon, you might consider covering your carpet with a cheap dhurry, which could be replaced after a few years.

Stairs impose the severest test of resilience on any form of covering, and should preferably be carpeted with extra heavy duty domestic or medium contract grades. An 80/20 wool/nylon carpet with high pile weight is usually the best choice. If you use stair rods you can leave a length of carpet tucked under each end and shift the carpet every two years or so to reduce the pattern of wear and tear.

Fitting, Underlays & Floor Preparation

Fitting a carpet requires skill and a number of specialized tools and is best left to professionals. Ideally the fitter should see the existing floor surface and agree with you exactly what remedial work, if any, needs to be done to it, and by whom, before the new carpet is laid.

If you are planning to carpet a relatively large area or cover more than one room with the same carpet, you may also need to consider whether it will be necessary to seam two pieces together. Electronic hot melt tape seaming provides almost invisible joins, but various other techniques can be used, depending on the type of carpet. When joining carpet at doorways, aluminium or brass anodized threshold strips are reasonably common, but can interrupt the sweep from room to room. Most carpets are now sold as broadloom, so that seaming is only required at doorways. If a join does prove necessary, make sure it runs with rather than across the direction of most traffic and that it lies away from the busiest areas. Remember, too, that you may need to order additional carpet to allow for matching patterns at joins. All these points should be discussed when obtaining quotations for the fitting.

Underlays are used with both fitted carpets and rugs to minimize the amount of abrasion caused by feet, furniture and grit, and thus preserve the carpet for longer. They will also reduce the effect of any slight unevenness in the structural floor beneath, improve comfort and provide additional sound- and noise-proofing. For safety reasons, you should consider placing underlay or double-sided sticky tape under rugs to stop them slipping on hard floors.

Underlays are available on the roll and are usually sold in widths of 120cm (4ft). The best come in the form of rubber crumb or sponge, although felt at least 8–9mm (around ⅜in) thick can also be used. Generally speaking, it is inadvisable to stick underlays to floors, although if used under rugs on highly polished surfaces they can be attached to the floor with double-sided tape. Some manufacturers produce carpets with integral underlays. These are more economical but less effective in preserving the carpet than separate ones, and this is less common than it used to be.

Proper preparation of the floor before laying is essential. This may entail replacing badly damaged boards, levelling out unevenness and punching down nails. If timber boards are in bad condition, the installer often recommends

ABOVE *To achieve a unified feeling without the expense of fitted carpet, an attractive hard-wearing woven runner is used for both hallway and stairs. Chunky stair rods provide strong horizontal lines to balance the vertical sweep of the carpet border.*

overlaying the floor with sheets of 3mm (⅛in) thick hardboard. This should be laid, rough side up, with staggered joints and allowing expansion gaps of approximately 2mm (just under ⅛in) at joins and 3–4mm (⅛in) around the perimeter of the room. If your existing floors are already covered with some kind of timber sheet, such as chipboard, this will offer a suitably smooth surface on which to lay carpet and is likely to need little preparation, except to sink protruding screw heads or flatten ridges at joints. Cement screeded floors should be completely dry, flat and firm. All wax or polish should be removed from stone or tiled floors. Existing sheet vinyl or tiles can be left in place provided that they are thoroughly stuck down.

ABOVE *The red carpet, with its suggestion of processions, is appropriate for this formal, almost ceremonial staircase. The unbroken sweep of carpet down the stairs and across the whole width of the small landing allows the eye to focus on the unusual architecture of the building and the carefully chosen symmetrical braziers, which add to the sense of ritual.*

Maintaining Carpets & Rugs

Since wear is caused by abrasion from feet, furniture and ingrained particles of grit, the most effective way to maintain your carpets is by fitting doormats and by encouraging people to leave their dirty shoes at the door. You should also ensure that rugs are lying flat so that ridges or folds are not exposed to excessive wear. In very wet weather you may wish to remove rugs temporarily from hallways or protect carpets with druggets of linen or canvas. Cups under the feet of heavy furniture will reduce marking from castors.

No matter how careful you are, carpets and rugs will inevitably need regular cleaning, ideally with a vacuum cleaner. Upright models are best for fitted carpet and should be used daily over several weeks on newly laid carpet to remove loose fibres resulting from the weaving and trimming processes. If allowed to remain in the carpet, these get trodden into the pile and matt it. On older carpets thorough vacuuming helps to lift a downtrodden pile as well as to remove grit. Rugs should be vacuumed on both sides to remove the dirt that sinks into the backing. Cleaners with brushes are suitable for carpets, but not for rugs.

As a last resort you can clean fitted carpets with an electric shampooer, provided they are not badly stained or very dirty, in which case it is wiser to employ a professional. Too frequent shampooing will remove the natural wool oils and increase future dirt retention. Allow the carpet to dry completely before any furniture is placed on it, but if this is impossible make sure that plastic cups are used under castors or metal legs. In all cases, follow the advice of the manufacturer, particularly for carpets protected with anti-staining treatments.

Rugs should always be washed by hand and never more than once a year. Rub gently with a stiff bristle brush on both sides over areas of about 1 square metre (1 square yard), blot so that the fibres do not become too wet, and finish by brushing the pile in its natural direction. Whatever cleaning technique you adopt, always try it out first on a small area on the back using a white cloth to see if the dyes are fast and make sure that the back of the rug is dried as carefully as the front. For stain removal, see page 182. If you are storing rugs for any length of time, spray them with an anti-moth liquid and keep them in a well-ventilated place.

Basic repairs can be done at home, although valuable rugs should always be taken to a specialist as unsatisfactory mending will affect their value. If a tuft or loop is caught and protrudes, try gently pulling some of the adjacent loops or cut it. Damage to fringes or selvedges on rugs should be mended as soon as possible, before continued abrasion spreads the problem over a wider area. A needle and thread can be used for simple repair jobs, but you should be sure to use the same type of yarn that has been used to make the rug. If you are unlucky enough to burn your carpet, the scorched ends of the natural fibres can be cut or rubbed away with abrasive paper or stone over a small area. Larger burns will have to be cut out and patched. Man-made fibres will melt and turn black if burned, so smokers should choose carpets with a high wool content.

The comfort of this stylish room derives from the mixture of elements and shows how traditional kelims, with their modern richness of colour and bold geometric patterns, can sit comfortably with furnishings of any period.

NATURAL FIBRES

Natural fibres combine many of the best qualities of other materials used for floor coverings and act as a perfect foil for any decorating scheme. They have become increasingly popular with designers over recent years and can look as attractive with the finest ornate antiques as with high-tech modern furniture or minimalist interiors.

Rushes, bracken and grass were among the first materials used to line the earth floors of human habitations in temperate areas. Readily available, they offered some insulation against cold and damp, could be sweet-smelling when trodden on and, in some cases, acted as insect repellants. Originally such materials were probably gathered in the neighbourhood and strewn loosely underfoot, to be swept up and discarded as they became worn and dirty. When woven or braided into mats, they formed a more durable surface, and archaeological discoveries suggest that this was done from very early times. In Somerset, where the boggy area known as the Levels still produces wetland materials such as willow and rush, matting has been found which dates back at least 3,000 years to before the Iron Age. By the fifteenth and sixteenth centuries country house records show that in Europe rush matting was in common use and was evidently being made in considerable quantities. An inventory dated 1622 records '120 yardes of Mat for my Ladyes chamber', and at around the same period rolls of matting were produced in a number of cottages in Pavenham, Bedfordshire, for flooring for London's Houses of Parliament.

Natural fibres of many other kinds have been harvested to make mats in most parts of the world, from tropical rainforests to the edges of the Arctic Circle. In Japan and Sarawak people have traditionally slept on reed and straw mats placed on the floor. Grass matting, some of it woven in fine and elaborate patterns, is widely used for a variety of purposes throughout Polynesia, as is coir, the coarse product of the coconut husk. Sisal is formed from the leaves of agave plants, which grow in Tanzania, China and Brazil, while the jute industry first developed in Eastern Bengal, where a hot moist climate favours the plants from which the fibre is made.

Although there are altogether around fifty types of fibre-producing plants woven into domestic matting in different cultures, the flooring generally sold in

This interior is bathed in the warmth of natural tones and textures; the honey colour of the natural-fibre floor is in harmony with the simple plain boarded walls and roof beams, and is complemented by the warm rust upholstery. The borders of the wood floor are highlighted by the crispness of the edge bindings on these natural 'rugs' and help to carry the eye through into the next room.

the West is based on sisal, coir, maize leaf, jute, abaca and grass, or combinations of these. Some suppliers of natural-fibre carpeting also stock carpets made of undyed wool or wool mixed with sisal and jute to combine the naturalness of fibres with the softness and durability of wool. Natural-fibre floor covering is available in broadloom, narrow roll and in mat or rug form, in which case the edges will be bound in natural, coloured or decorative tape, or even in leather. In their undyed state, most natural fibres fall within a fairly limited palette of browns, creams and pale yellow-greens, but several manufacturers use dyed fibres to produce flooring in strong plain shades or in patterned combinations of colour. Backings tend to be made of latex.

Rush Matting

Rushes grow all over the world in temperate climates, and are pliable when wet but brittle when dry. Soft and silky, they will fade to a uniform muted brown, and today are used mainly to make medieval-type plaited mats. Long hand-plaited strips approximately 9cm (3¾in) wide are sewn together to give a covering as large as you wish. These mats have a very traditional feel but they are not very hard-wearing. If laid in areas of heavy traffic they should be protected and rugs are an ideal and complementary overlay. Great care should be taken when moving furniture over them as they are easily damaged. They are therefore more suitable for areas such as studies or bedrooms than dining or living rooms. They are also extremely useful on floors which may be slightly damp, such as old stone flags, where, providing there is ventilation, they will survive well. Indeed an intermittent light sprinkling of water will help them to last longer, because they become frail and brittle if too dry.

ABOVE *Rush flooring completes a comfortable and assured fusion of elements both modern and traditional. It harmonizes with the old panelled door and heavy wooden beams, while the four-poster bed is built in a modern style. The silkiness of rush adds sparkle and is suitably soft underfoot.*

OPPOSITE *This interior derives its character from the strong contrast between the heavily textured grass and the shiny dark dado. Extending under the dark painted bath, the grass makes the bath appear almost to float.*

Grass

The grass used for flooring grows in moist conditions similar to those in paddy fields and is therefore impervious to water. This means that it will not take dyes and is available only in its natural colours: greens when fresh, fading to pale yellows and honey browns, sometimes with a green tinge. However, the same characteristic also ensures that of all the natural grass-like fibres it is the most resistant to stains and wet dirt. Produced in simple heavy-weave patterns, grass is sometimes also available with a coloured weft thread made from a different fibre giving a hint of red, blue or black.

Grass flooring generally comes in widths of 4m (13ft). Heavier grass fibres are also woven into squares, usually measuring 30×30cm (1×1ft) and about 9mm (⅜in) thick. These are sewn together to form mats in a wide variety of sizes, which can be joined to provide a handsome overall covering for a large area. The fibres have a delicious scent of hay when new. Grass flooring is suitable for medium traffic and should be avoided in busy hallways or similar areas, or in places where furniture is likely to be dragged over it, such as dining rooms. To provide grass with additional strength, it is sometimes combined with hemp, a fibre similar to jute in its resilience.

A selection of bouclé coir with wefts in different colours.

Coir

Produced mainly in India and in some Pacific regions, coir is made from the short strong brown fibres of the coconut husk. Its name is derived from the Malay kayar, or 'cord'. Coir is rough to the touch and extremely resistant to abrasion. For these reasons it has traditionally been used for doormats, but more recently it has been woven into a very hard-wearing carpet and is ideal in parts of the house where there is likely to be a good deal of traffic.

Coir is dyed and woven in a range of single-coloured patterns, including simple plaited and herringbone weaves. It is also available in a range of bright colours woven into diamond or basketweave patterns, but these colours will be affected by strong sunlight. Coir is supplied in economical narrow rolls either 70cm (28½in) or 1m (39½in) in width, which are ideal for hallways and passages, as well as in broadloom 4m (13ft) wide and 50×50cm (20×20in) tiles for larger areas. Larger retailers also offer bound mats and runners in almost any size.

Jute

The plants from which jute is obtained are tall annuals, which grow in temperate and subtropical regions in many parts of the world, particularly in India, Bangladesh and Pakistan. The fibres are extracted from the stems by hand after soaking. Of all the natural fibres cultivated commercially, only cotton is produced on a larger scale.

Jute has been used for centuries to make cheap sacking and ropes because of its combination of strength and softness, and it is now woven on a vast scale as backing for carpet and rugs of all types. Originally jute was made mainly into ropes, paper and cloth, but manufacture expanded significantly during the nineteenth century when its versatility became apparent in the West, and tons of the raw material were imported into Britain for mechanized spinning and weaving. Jute is also combined with other fibres, including wool, to make a range of rugs and matting.

Jute is the softest of the natural fibres and the best-quality threads can be almost silky, with a natural lustre. It is not, however, very hard-wearing when subject to abrasion and should be avoided in areas of heavy use. Available in plain, herringbone and bouclé as well as multicoloured weaves, jute is sold in widths of 70cm (28in) and 4m (13ft) broadloom and as bound mats and runners in a wide range of sizes. Like coir, jute when dyed or bleached can be affected by direct sunlight.

OPPOSITE *Jute and coir come in a range of interesting weaves and in dyed, bleached and natural plain colours and combinations of colour to complement many furnishing styles. The selection shown here gives some indication of the available choice and* includes: CLOCKWISE FROM TOP LEFT *standard coir hand-woven weave in natural coconut colour; luxury coir diamond contrast weave; textured jute; North Sea green jute designed for borders; ribbed jute; two-coloured tweed weave jute.*

Sisal

Less rough to the touch than coir, sisal is nevertheless a hard-wearing fibre. It is made from the spiky leaves of a subtropical bush which is grown commercially, mainly in Tanzania, China and Brazil. The fibre is separated from the flesh of the leaf by immersion in water, and because the leaves can grow up to 160cm (over 5ft) long, the resulting threads are eminently suitable for weaving.

Sisal is strong but supple and, while rougher than jute, is certainly soft enough to be used in bedrooms. It is generally woven into ribbed, bouclé and herringbone patterns. The ribbed weaves, especially in two colours, and the herringbone weave with a darker weft, will make a strong directional statement. An extensive range of more decorative weaves which mix natural colours with threads of greys, reds, pinks and greens is also available. When three rustic colours are used in a coarse weave the result is reminiscent of rough Scottish or Irish tweed. Sisal comes in a range of plain colours to suit most decorating schemes; for a calm, understated backdrop there are the restful neutrals in shades of natural golden browns or darker honey browns. To add a touch of contemporary drama to large expanses of floor, for instance in a warehouse or period conversion, there are plain dyed strong colours, including heart-stopping reds, greens, blues and black. Suppliers can provide sisal in runners of 70cm (28in) or in widths of 4m (13ft) broadloom and in edge-bound scatter rugs up to 360×240cm (12×8ft).

FROM TOP *Sisal in herringbone weave with brown weft; three-coloured plaid; denim blue bouclé; gold.*

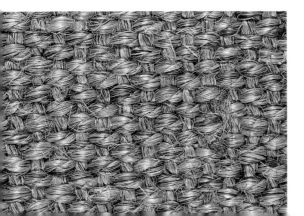

BELOW *Sisal is also successfully woven as a mix with natural undyed wool to give a soft but heavily textured weave. These are three examples of a sisal/wool mix.*

OPPOSITE *In a Mediterranean room a honey-coloured sisal in a bouclé weave acts as a necessary foil to the intense theatricality of the sofa and the rococo curves of the star-studded shrine.*

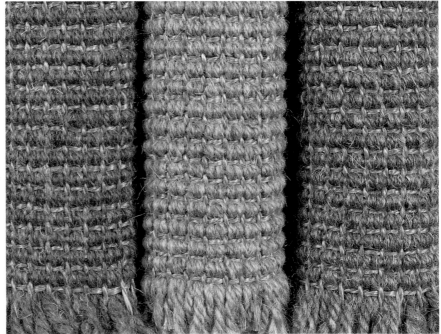

BELOW *A small interior is made to feel spacious by the extension of the ribbed jute mats into the room beyond, providing a warm contrast with the plain bare walls. Laying the natural floor covering to leave a dark border of wood helps create the traditional style picked up in the furnishings and makes a definite edge to the space, as there is no skirting on the walls.*

RIGHT *This carefully created interior shows neutral flooring at its best. The grass acts as a quiet background for the sophisticated and decorative furnishing arrangement, allowing the ornate blue chairs to stand out crisply while matching their rush seats. The ribbed weave of the mat runs around in a square to create subtle radiating diagonal lines at the joints, emphasizing the centre of the room and the focus on the round table.*

Tatami Mats

The Japanese tatami mat is perhaps one of the most enduring examples of a natural, locally produced floor covering that is perfectly integrated into its architectural, cultural and decorative contexts. Indeed the dimensions of rooms in a traditional Japanese house are fixed according to the size of a standard tatami mat, which imparts a sense of harmony and ordered continuity to the whole building. Although their warm yellow tones harmonize with the subtle natural tones of the timber, bamboo and paper traditionally used in Japan, these mats can look just as good in contemporary Western interiors, particularly where furniture is kept to a minimum.

Originally the sizes in which tatami mats were made varied from region to region, but they have now been fixed at about 2×1m (approximately 6×3ft). They are around 5cm (2in) thick and are formed from a composite of reed matting over a core of rice straw, the layers connected by rows of stitches which give the mats their characteristic ribbed quality. A tape binding keeps the edges firm. Placed edge to edge, tatami mats are comfortably soft to walk on, are good insulators, and serve also for sitting and sleeping. While easily cleaned by vacuuming or wiping with a damp cloth, they stain readily, and are not fire resistant. In Japan they are used to floor every room except wash rooms and external balconies. Tatami mats are available from a few specialist shops. They are not suitable for use under furniture with legs.

Wood Twine Matting

Similar in their simplicity to the Japanese tatami mat, wood twine mats are derived from pulp and are essentially paper. They come in a range of natural colours as well as in subtle shades of earthy russet, green and grey, and more striking combinations of natural and black or rust, some with coloured borders. These coverings bring together the honest simplicity of traditional rush mat with the sophistication of elegant and restrained designs. They are, however, relatively costly and would be inappropriate in rooms likely to get messy such as children's bedrooms and playrooms.

Wood twine mats are available in standard sizes ranging from 90×200cm (3ft×6ft8in) up to almost room size, 250×350cm (8ft3in×11ft8in). You can also order sizes up to any length with a maximum width of 250cm(8ft3in). Although only 5mm (less than ¼in) thick, they are laid on a thin rubber underlay and therefore feel quite soft underfoot. Like other natural-fibre floors, these mats stain, but, unlike many others, they can be washed in warm water with a neutral detergent. Use a brush to scrub the mat gently in the direction of the weft, rinse thoroughly in clean water and leave to dry, avoiding direct sunlight. Note, however, that the mats will shrink some 2–3% with the first wash. Spilled grease or similar stains can be removed by scraping. It is possible to apply one of the proprietary stain repellents, which can be renewed in time, and suppliers are currently developing stain resistant treatments. One of the particular advantages of these mats is that they will not deteriorate with damp and are therefore suitable for older properties with stone floors.

OPPOSITE *The calm of this interior comes from the lack of clutter and the simple regularity of each of the materials: the order of the tatami floor mats, the linear pattern of the timber ceiling beams and boards, and the rough texture of the brick walls, all of which have been left undecorated in a modern way. Because the mats act as seats as well as floor covering, there is no need for furniture.*

BELOW *Discreet pattern can be seen to best advantage in natural materials such as these wood twine mats. Crisp and definite when examined from close to, the patterns will merge at a distance into a subtle overall mottled tone.*

Unusual Fibres

A number of other plants have leaves and stems large enough to make their fibres suitable for weaving. Abaca comes from Manila hemp, a relative of the banana tree which grows in the Philippines, South East Asia and Central America. The coarse outer fibres of the leafstalk can be up to 5m (16ft) long. Although softer to the touch than sisal or coir, abaca is one of the strongest natural fibres and is woven into extremely durable, heavily ribbed mats in neutral grey and pale honey tones, measuring 180×270cm (6×9ft), 240×300cm (8×10ft) and 270×360cm (9×12ft). In the United States, small mats made of traditional corn husks are available from specialist shops.

Selection & Design

Natural coverings have a host of qualities to recommend them. They are light and reflective, and although their softness is not that of carpet, it is sufficient – particularly in the case of jute and grass – to provide warmth underfoot, to absorb sound and to act as a good thermal insulator. The natural rich golden browns of most undyed fibres create a neutral and yet textured background for any decorative style and allow you to use a wide range of palettes for walls and fabrics. When combined with natural-fibre flooring, strong bright primary colours will make a room feel upbeat and fresh, while darker earthy terracottas, browns and ochres will suggest a more mellow, almost Mediterranean atmosphere. Alternatively these fibres go well with quieter, more recessive shades of bleached blues and greys for walls and undyed calico and cotton for soft furnishings, in a Scandinavian style.

Antiques or traditional furniture in dark timbers, with richer upholstery and curtains, also sit very comfortably with natural floor coverings. Indeed, the National Trust still furnishes many of its historic British houses with rush matting made of simple plaits sewn together as they have been for centuries. You can achieve a similar traditional effect by cutting many kinds of natural-fibre flooring to about 60cm (2ft) less than the size of the room all round and staining the uncovered floorboards dark to contrast with the covering. To protect the edges of the carpet, either turn them under and tape them, if they are thin and flexible, or bind them. A range of decorative bindings is available, although plain hessian is least distracting to the eye.

To create a strong sense of continuous space, you can lay natural floor covering throughout a small house or flat, and give focus to specific areas with a bright woollen or cotton rug. Although pleasing in isolation and suitable for specific decorating schemes, the kinds of natural-fibre carpeting that come in multicoloured striped or flecked patterns should be used with care. The dyed bright colours used to create the designs may look harsh and strident when laid over large areas and can become overdominant.

Natural floors can look particularly good in large farmhouse kitchens but it is unwise to lay them in the area directly in front of the kitchen units or stove. The coarse strands of fibre trap dirt and are difficult to clean. If you use natural fibres in the bathroom you should be careful not to drench the floor with water.

ABOVE *Abaca rugs, here shown in shades of gold, black and a natural-black mix, are woven in a distinctive ribbed pattern.*

OPPOSITE *The coir carpet contributes to the strong sculptural quality of this staircase, in which the sensuous lines of handrail, balustrade and low wall are picked up by the dark line of the edge binding on the carpet. The carpet is given emphasis by the strong herringbone weave, which contrasts with the smooth elements. The simple strength of this interior is increased by the way the coir has been chosen to match the same colour palette as the stone walls.*

Laying

Before fitting, natural-fibre flooring should be laid out across the space, cut to approximately 5cm (2in) larger than the room size and then left to acclimatize for a minimum of 48 hours, ideally with the room at its anticipated normal temperature. Make sure that any new cement or plaster work is completely dry beforehand or it will increase the room's humidity.

It is normally recommended that natural coverings with a latex backing are stuck down, as otherwise they tend to shrink and move. Easy-peel adhesives are available for glueing, but I always try to avoid sticking anything to a floor and have laid a large studio area loose except for the occasional strip of double-sided tape, and have not experienced any significant movement. You should, however, take note of the manufacturer's instructions about laying so that you do not risk forfeiting any guarantees.

Underlays are not strictly necessary with most natural-fibre floors but, as for all types of carpet, any additional layer will prolong the life of the carpet and improve the level of comfort. Jute-backed coverings should always be laid on underlay, preferably of felt, and can be fitted with gripper rods on stairs in the same way as woollen carpet. If you want a truly authentic traditional look, they should be tacked down using non-rusting tacks or U-shaped staples, which are almost invisible. Old-fashioned rush matting is always laid loose and will also benefit from an underlay. Although it is possible to use heat-sensitive tape for joints and seaming, sewing gives a more lasting finish. Avoid using metal threshold strips at doorways and edges since these look incongruous against the natural fibres. Cuts made to accommodate fittings should be turned under and sewn, or bound with hessian and stapled.

Cleaning & Maintenance

The relative difficulty of keeping natural-fibre floors clean is the one disadvantage that might weigh against them. Unlike wool, these plant fibres are not oily and do not shed stains naturally. Since many undyed natural floor coverings are also light in colour, they will tend to show the dirt more easily and particular care must be taken to ensure that they are not exposed to mud and other soiling. The most stain-resistant is grass, but it is unfortunately amongst the least durable, and along with other natural fibres is likely to have a limited life unless protected in areas of very heavy wear – entrance halls, for example. If you do want to use natural fibres in places where they are likely to be exposed to considerable traffic, you can try arranging the floor with a sacrificial strip which can be replaced when it wears out.

For general cleaning use a vacuum cleaner with good suction. Some suppliers sell stain-resistant carpet which has been treated to minimize the effect of spills without changing the texture. By and large these treatments are effective but they do wear off eventually and your carpet may need retreatment. Most spills can be dealt with by dabbing the floor with a wet sponge as quickly as possible. Lumps of dirt can be removed with a stiff brush, brushing in the direction of the weave.

This lovely verandah is made comfortably inviting by the warmth of the herringbone-weave jute runners, which help to create the feeling of an inside-outside space. The lightness of the natural tone reflects golden light into an interior which would have been much darker had the underlying brown tiles remained uncovered. Loose laid, the runners can be rolled up if wind threatens to bring in the rain.

SHEET FLOORING

Until the middle of the nineteenth century there was only one floor covering other than carpet that could be rolled out to cover hard or cold structural floors: the hand-painted floorcloths found in homes throughout America and Britain from the eighteenth century onwards. These were painstakingly made by hand-painting pieces of stretched canvas with as many as seven coats of oil paint. Floorcloths were much more practical than carpet, since they could be wiped or mopped down, and they were produced in designs ranging from bold geometric patterns to imitations of marble or tiles.

The practicality and universal appeal of floorcloths prompted the development and commercial production of linoleum near London in 1864. This new material was described in the American Sears Roebuck catalogue of the 1890s as being 'very much like oil cloth except that there is ground cork in its composition which makes it heavier, more durable and much softer to walk on.' Linoleum found favour not only among the buying public, but also among designers of the early twentieth century, who sought to sweep away what they saw as the stuffy ornateness of Victorian interiors with their impractical, dust-collecting carpets. Bauhaus and other innovative designers used linoleum in either plain colours or bold patterns – styles that have again come into vogue over the last few years.

The qualities that made linoleum attractive – its ease of use, comfort and comparative inexpensiveness – led in turn to the development during the 1930s and 1940s of other sheet floor coverings. Synthetic rubber flooring, which was tough and virtually maintenance free, became a popular choice for factories and cinemas. The high-tech styles of the 1960s, which celebrated industrial materials for their utility and robustness, brought this kind of flooring into people's homes and encouraged manufacturers to make rubber sheet in a range of bright colours and with a variety of raised patterns. Improvements in production processes and pigments have also benefited linoleum and PVC, and the limited range of dull colours traditionally associated with these materials has been superseded by a more extensive range – today they offer great potential for

The early twentieth-century style of the fittings and furniture determined the bold pattern of this linoleum floor, in which the contrasting cream and dark blue elements mirror the contrast between the pale walls and cupboards and the dark furniture. The spaciousness of this loose-fit kitchen with its free-standing cupboards is emphasized by the way the floor pattern runs beneath the units. Although the development of synthetic materials made linoleum seem old-fashioned, it has recently regained its popularity due to the development of a range of modern designs.

creating practical and attractive floors in the home.

Recently, many designers have exploited the opportunities offered by the strong colours and accurate computer-controlled cutting of sheet materials. Whether in plain or subtly marbled shades, linoleum, vinyl and rubber provide practical, durable and easily maintained surfaces. The fact that they are suitable for wet areas means that sheet floors can be laid through an entire house, sweeping from one room to another to suggest a sense of extension and space which works especially well in open-plan accommodation. Linoleums and cork also provide some of the natural warmth and feel of wood, which allows you to consider laying them in living rooms as well as service areas. Although not as soft as foam-backed vinyl, linoleum is available with a cork backing which gives it additional thermal and sound-reducing qualities.

Now that vinyls and linoleums are made in so many colours and textures, with some manufacturers boasting up to one hundred choices in their range, it is possible to develop your own designs using precut or specially ordered pieces and to achieve an even greater variety than that offered by ceramic tiles. Regular geometric repeats, large freehand abstract shapes and figures, and crisp and delicate borders can all be made from sheet materials. Or you may prefer the more traditional furnishing styles associated with hard floors: simple chequerboards of alternating colours or plain squares with inset key squares.

Linoleum

Named from the Latin words describing its main constituents – *linum*, meaning flax, and *oleum*, meaning oil – linoleum's obvious usefulness made it extremely popular when it was first produced in the mid-nineteenth century. Nothing like it had existed before, and by the end of the century it was being made by a number of manufacturers, some of whom are still the main producers today. Warmer and softer than stone, ceramic and timber floors, it nevertheless offers much of their durability and ease of maintenance.

The production of lineolum involves a complex and lengthy sequence of processes. Many of its ingredients occur naturally and are of two types: a binder, which is a mixture of linseed oil and resin (usually from pine trees), and a filler, which can be cork, wood flour (ground wood waste), whiting (a form of chalk) and pigments. These are rolled into a sheet, bonded with a hessian backing and then toughened under heat, after which the face is coated. Although the cork traditionally helped give linoleum its flexibility and warmth, together with the linseed oil it was originally responsible for its dark and sombre tones. Advances in binder and colour technology have since made it possible to manufacture linoleum in much brighter shades, which has contributed to its return to fashion.

Precut linoleum shapes allow you to have inlay patterns of unlimited scope. These can be made up in customized designs of relative complexity. An economical alternative is to choose from a standard range of patterns for borders and centre features. They are normally cut in the factory and supplied positioned in place with an adhesive film on the face which is removed after fixing to the floor; or they can be supplied as separate pieces to be fitted like a jigsaw.

Linoleum is generally resistant to staining from solvents and oils, to impact,

CLOCKWISE FROM TOP LEFT *A modern update of a 'palazzo' floor with contrasting key squares and a diamond border; a classical chequerboard pattern with key squares (both suitable for a living room); a black and blue chequerboard with inlaid stars, inspired by the floors of Renaissance churches; a trompe-l'oeil tumbling blocks pattern (both suitable for a bedroom); a gingham design suitable for a kitchen or bathroom; a chequerboard with spot tiles suitable for a conservatory or garden room.*

abrasion, scarring and cigarette burns, and because the colour is not confined to the surface but goes right through the material even the worst damage is hardly visible. The oxidized linseed oil and wood flour make it a relatively good insulant and give it some resilience.

Now that there is so much interest in naturally based products and the colour and design have improved, linoleum has lost its dull old-fashioned image and has come to be accepted as an extremely versatile floor material for use throughout the house. Hygienic and easy to clean, it can be used in wet areas if joints are seam-welded to skirtings and accessories. Because it is made from natural materials, perfect consistency from one batch to another is almost impossible to achieve; but this variety in appearance can be seen as a virtue, not a drawback.

Linoleum comes in rolls 2m (6ft 6in) wide or as tiles 50×50cm (19¾×19¾in) or 33×33cm (13×13in) square, and in thicknesses of 2, 2.5 or 3.2mm (½₂, ¹⁄₁₀ or ⅛in). Premade borders are available in strips, often measuring 100×10cm (39½×4in). Key squares are made for combining with clipped corner squares, allowing you to create the kinds of designs typically found in marble and ceramic floors. Linoleum may at first have a slightly yellow blush, but this will disappear after it has been exposed to light. Where floors are particularly uneven or where additional sound reduction is required, it is possible to buy linoleum with a cork back or to lay the linoleum on top of cork sheet.

Vinyl Sheet & Tile

The word 'vinyl' is shorthand for polyvinyl chloride, or PVC, a synthetic material developed from petroleum derivatives. Although thermoplastic tiles containing PVC were first made in America during World War II, flexible PVC sheet and tiles, as we know them, did not come onto the market until the late 1950s. The production process is relatively simple. A dough-like mixture is put while hot through enormous rollers to create a sheet usually 2, 2.5 or 3.2mm (½₂, ¹⁄₁₀ or ⅛in) thick. It is then cooled and cut either into roll lengths or tiles.

As with linoleum, which PVC was intended to replace, this process initially imposed limitations on the colour and patterning that could be introduced into the material, but in recent years technical developments have made it possible to increase the range of colours and textures enormously, from the traditional marbled and veined appearance imitating stone, to speckled effects and brighter plain shades.

Vinyl floor coverings are available in a number of distinct forms, all of which have different characteristics. These include plain sheet and tiles, clear PVC-covered sheet, foam-backed sheet and slip-resisting sheet and tiles. Sheet flooring is either homogeneous, in which case the colour and pattern run through the whole thickness of the material to give it exceptional longevity, or heterogeneous, in which case the colour and pattern exist only on a thin wearing surface which is attached to a plain backing.

Traditionally not as durable as homogeneous vinyls, today the durability of the better grade heterogeneous materials is just as good for normal domestic use. The advantage of the heterogeneous production process is that other

BELOW *This bold pattern of squares, circles and fluid curves demonstrates how a floor made of cut vinyl can act as the main feature in an otherwise plain and unadorned bathroom.*

Many manufacturers offer a custom-made design and cutting service, ranging from the adaptation of existing patterns in almost any combination of colours, to designs made to individual specifications, with inlays of family crests or even names.

ABOVE LEFT *A cobalt-blue tile pattern with insets of yellow ochre fleur-de-lys in a jet lattice and border provides striking accents in a small hallway.*

ABOVE AND LEFT *To add interest to an otherwise plain floor, a comparatively simple swirl can be as successful as a more complex shell design.*

materials can be incorporated into the structure, notably glass-fibre reinforcing. This makes the sheet more stable and means that in many circumstances it can be laid flat and simply trimmed with a knife to fit the space and does not need to be glued down. You are therefore able to replace the vinyl easily without creating a sticky layer that is almost impossible to remove – a great help when you are renovating a house or if room arrangements are likely to change.

The manufacturers of vinyl do make distinctions between contract and domestic vinyls. Those classified as being for domestic use, most commonly cushioned or foam-backed vinyls, are relatively inexpensive, but they tend to have a thin wearing layer which gives them a more limited life span than contract kinds resulting in the kind of discoloration seen in areas of localized constant wear, particularly in front of kitchen sinks and appliances. Ordinary domestic grade tiles are consequently not advisable for kitchens or other places where they will be subject to heavy use.

Although many floor-laying companies make no mention of this, some manufacturers recommend using contract grade vinyls in kitchens. These are specifically made to retain their appearance with heavy wear and are available in a much wider range of colours and patterns. While they are more expensive than the domestic types, the total cost difference over the area of a room is unlikely to be great, and they will obviously need replacing less often.

Sheet vinyl generally comes in rolls 2, 3 and 4m (6ft 6in, 9ft 9in and 13ft) wide or in tiles either 30×30cm (11¾×11¾in) or 50×50cm (19¾×19¾in) square. Less common today, but still in use, are semi-flexible PVC tiles, which tend to be more economical to install and can be laid on ground floors with bituminous adhesives to keep a certain amount of damp at bay. They should not, however, be regarded as a substitute for a proper damp-proof membrane as a means of keeping the floor dry.

A wide range of designs, patterns, borders and inlays is available in vinyl, either in tile or in special precut forms. If you give a colour-coded design to the manufacturers, they will produce a set of precut pieces to be either heat- or solvent-welded together and fitted on site. Plain vinyl, being smooth and synthetic, tends to have an institutional feel and is probably best used to create a 'high-tech' look or in service areas, where it will provide a simple unobtrusive floor covering that is easy to clean.

Durable and easy to maintain, vinyl generally retains its appearance well. However, since it is dense and somewhat hard, it is not a good thermal or sound insulant by itself. There is little to choose between vinyl and linoleum as far as their functional characteristics and possible uses are concerned, although linoleum is somewhat softer and more resilient. One of the advantages of vinyl is that manufacturers produce an extensive range of covings, edge trims and non-slip nosings for stair treads in this material, all of which are welded together to provide a seamless and totally impervious floor, which is ideal in wet areas, such as shower rooms and utility rooms.

In a farmhouse close to the coast, a simple chequerboard of vinyl floor tiles in blue and white gives the kitchen a traditional, slightly nautical feel and acts as a fresh, light background to the solid, painted chairs and a large limed dresser.

OPPOSITE *A bespoke design in vinyl makes a practical yet classical floor for this utilitarian space. The subtle tones of a traditional limestone floor, complete with darker inset key squares, are picked up in the grey cupboards and counterpointed by a splash of colour in the stained glass of the half-glazed doors.*

BELOW *Linoleum in three different colours is used here to recreate an ornate 'tumbling block' design of a kind usually found in marble floors. It adds a traditional touch to an otherwise modern furnishing scheme, the two shades of brown in the floor reflecting the two browns of the unusual wooden table.*

Clear PVC-faced Vinyls

Clear PVC-faced vinyls have a sandwich construction consisting of a vinyl backing, a visual layer providing the pattern and colour and a durable clear PVC wearing layer to protect the visual layer. Made until recently by only one manufacturer, these vinyls are available in a wide variety of very attractive designs and have brought attractive, good-quality, low-maintenance PVC floors into many character interiors. Many of the designs emulate other materials, such as timber strips, parquet, marble, slate, tiles, brick or even beaten metal, and they are matched by a correspondingly large range of inlay borders, motifs and patterns. In some cases the patterns and designs are transferred photographically and are remarkably realistic, so much so that it is only by touching the floor that you can distinguish it from the real material. This effect is heightened by the fact that some of the ranges are sold in pieces of a size similar to those of the hard floors being simulated, whether they are strips of timber, random planks or blocks of parquet to be glued down. Tiles come in around ten sizes, from 11.4×11.4cm (4¼×4¼in) up to 91.5×91.5cm (36×36in) depending on the design. This material is stain-resistant, hard-wearing and extremely dense, but has little effective sound-reduction capacity. Faced vinyl can be as expensive to buy as some of the real materials it is attempting to imitate and is intended to offer the visual characteristics of natural hard floors combined with the advantages of impervious, stain-resistant, easy to clean, and marginally quieter and warmer coverings. It is worth remembering, however, that in common with all vinyl floorings, faced vinyls will be badly affected by cigarette burns and by contact with certain other materials, such as rubber mats, some types of plastic or rubber furniture cups or plastic castors, shoe polish and paints.

Foam-backed Vinyl

Vinyl sheet with either a soft foam or felt backing was originally developed to minimize noise in such places as hospitals, but it can be extremely useful in the home, where it provides a soft but impervious, low-maintenance flooring for kitchens and bathrooms and is particularly suitable for laying on concrete. The resilient backing adds significant softness, which absorbs impact, deadening sound as well as providing extra comfort underfoot. The range of colours and patterns available is almost as extensive as for sheet vinyl, but cushion-backed versions do not come in tile form. Foam backings for domestic vinyls vary in thickness from 1.5 to 3mm (¹⁄₁₆to ⅛in), with a 5mm (¼in) layer available for use on sports floors. This means that total thicknesses vary between 3.5 and 7mm (⅛ and just over ¼in). The foam-backed type is ideal where a wet service area is located above quieter rooms. In bathrooms, for example, it will make an excellent background for a colourful mat or dhurry if you choose one of the neutral beige/cream or pale grey tones, in which the veining is not too strongly coloured. Felt-backed vinyls come in a wide range of colours and patterns, many of them imitating ceramic floors. They are available in rolls up to 2m (6ft 6in) wide, so joints in wet areas can be kept to a minimum. These vinyls should only be laid on solid ground floors which incorporate a damp-proof membrane.

PVC-faced vinyl tiles come in a wide range of different patterns, some produced photographically, others offering realistic imitations of other materials. CLOCKWISE FROM TOP LEFT *Weathered elm parquet; blue roman marble; sand; white Gregorian marble; water; mosaic centre motif.*

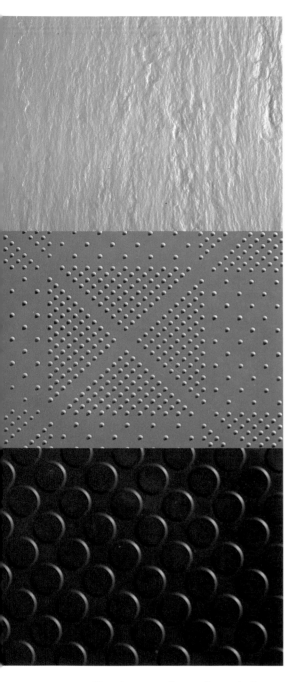

Rubber sheet is made in a choice of colours and patterns. FROM TOP *slated finish; mini stud pattern; large studs; slate structure.*

Slip-resistant Vinyl

Slip-resistant vinyl is available in both sheet and tile forms, and in a number of finishes, ranging from slightly gritty surfaces, which include carborundum dust, to heavily ridged and studded textures. Patterns tend to be limited to plainer colours, with the flecks of the non-slip ingredient more or less evident. In some the flecks show white against dark backgrounds, in others they are similar in colour to the background. Developed essentially for use in large commercial kitchens and factories, slip-resistant vinyls can be useful in the home if you are particularly concerned about safety in wet areas. However, their necessary roughness means that they are not ideal for rooms in which children are likely to be playing on the floor.

Rubber Flooring

Natural rubber sheet was first made during the nineteenth century. The rubber flooring most used today is manufactured mainly in America, Germany and Italy from synthetic by-products of the petrochemical industry. It is impervious, virtually unaffected by small spills of chemicals or oils and has excellent resistance to cigarette burns. Industrial-quality rubber sheet is obtainable in black only from industrial supply catalogues and comes both in plain form and in an extensive range of patterns, which include wide and narrow ribs, herringbone, chequerplate and wavy ribs, and a variety of studs. It is mainly sold in sheets 122cm (48in) wide or in tiles measuring 50×50cm (19¾×19¾in) square, but other sizes are available. It is also possible to buy interlocking tiles for loose laying. Thicknesses vary from 2.5mm (under ⅛in) up to as much as 3cm (1¼in). When used in the home, industrial-quality rubber can make practical and striking floors with a high-tech, no-nonsense appearance.

The plain brightly coloured rubber flooring designed for the domestic market comes in a smaller range of patterns, usually round and square studs, small pimple textures and ribs, and in thicknesses of either 2.5 or 4mm (just under and just over ⅛in). These are ideal in bathrooms, utility areas, entrance halls and playrooms. Rubber flooring has many of the waterproof and practical qualities of linoleum and PVC, but tends to be softer, quieter and warmer to the touch, as well as more hard-wearing. The studded or ribbed versions are among the most slip-resistant sheet floorings available. They can, however, be more difficult to keep clean and the lighter colours in particular require a more stringent maintenance regime than linoleum or vinyl. A range of rubber flooring with flecked, textured or slate-like riven surfaces is available. Closer in appearance to vinyl, these kinds do not offer the same slip resistance as the studded patterns and are not recommended for laying in wet areas. Rubber flooring is excellent on staircases, for which matching and integrated nosings can be bought. It can usefully be combined with other materials, too, perhaps as a strip in front of kitchen units where carpet or timber has been used for an adjacent dining space. Since rubber can be bought in the form of small mats and is so thin, it serves particularly well as a loosely laid, temporary mat by a garden door or can be kept in front of a workbench for easy lifting and cleaning.

Cork

Cork comes from the bark of the cork oak tree, which grows primarily in the Western Mediterranean, and the bulk of supplies are exported from Portugal, Spain and Algeria. Attempts to introduce the tree to California have met with only limited success. The bark, usually between 2.5 and 5cm (1 and 2in) thick, is stripped off every nine years or so, after which the tree is left alone to generate a new layer. Cork's unique combination of insulating properties, imperviousness and soft flexibility are the result of its structure of fatty materials, in which each cell is a watertight compartment. This is thought to be a natural adaptive characteristic designed to protect the tree against harsh drying summer winds.

Most cork floor tiles are formed from granules of the bark bonded with polyurethane resin, although some are made from slices taken directly from the bark. Any wear in a cork floor is likely to be due to abrasion, which means that it is important to apply some kind of protective sealant to the tiles. Some tiles can be bought with a prefinished layer of clear PVC, lacquer or acrylic varnish, which makes them ready for use; others are supplied in an unfinished state and will require sealing after they have been laid. Remember, when buying unsealed tiles, that varnishing is likely to darken the natural colour.

Cork can be obtained in a reasonably wide range of different colours, from natural honey browns to tints of pale beige, ivory, red, green, blue and grey, as well as dark-grey charcoal and browny red. On some tiles you may find obvious markings, with visible grain patterns or chips of cork apparently running in lines from one side to the other. Since there is a natural colour variation in the material, there are also likely to be differences from one pack to another. To avoid ending up with unattractive patches of darker and lighter tiles, you should aim to lay tiles of different batches randomly around the room. A limited number of printed coloured designs and patterns can also be obtained, and if you wish to decorate your own cork floor, you can paint or stencil unfinished tiles yourself before sealing.

Like carpet, cork is produced in several grades: domestic, which is 3mm (⅛in) thick; heavy domestic, also 3mm (⅛in) thick; and contract, 4.8mm (between ⅛ and ¼in) thick. Tile sizes are usually 30cm (just under 12in) square in Europe or 30.5cm (12in) square in the USA, although it is also possible to buy composite planks measuring 90×18.5cm (around 36×7in) and 9mm (⅜in) thick. The planks consist of a plywood or particle board base layer, a compressible cork inner core, a veneer of better-quality cork and a clear semi-matt PVC wearing layer. While thinner tiles usually have to be glued to the floor with a special adhesive, composite planks are tongued and grooved so they can be glued to each other instead of being fixed to the sub-floor. They are laid over a sheet cork underlay which accommodates irregularities in the subfloor as well as creating a sound-absorbing floating floor. Certain better-quality tiles have lipped edges which interlock when laid to seal the joints. If you are laying cork on concrete and are particularly anxious about warmth, you might consider using industrial cork sheeting, which is thicker than standard floor tiles. It is difficult to obtain and is harder to lay and seal but may well be worth the additional trouble.

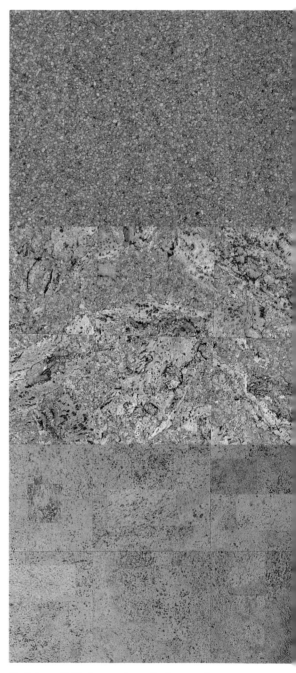

Cork is available in a variety of colours and grain patterns to suit different rooms. FROM TOP *Natural; accent; land; sky.*

Floorcloths

Sometimes known in America as oilcloths, floorcloths were very common until the mid-nineteenth century, when they were largely superseded by linoleum Recently their attractions have been rediscovered, and they now offer the opportunity to add a very personal touch to your home.

The best-quality floorcloths were, and still are, carefully crafted work made of single unjoined pieces of canvas. When imports from England stopped after the War for Independence, the extensive demand in America for these floor coverings prompted house- and ship-painters and interior decorating firms to start making them there. Canvas is stretched over a frame or pegged to the floor and then coated with up to seven background coats of oil-based paints on each side. The final design is then painted freehand or stencilled onto the surface.

Now that labour costs are so high, manufactured sheet flooring such as linoleum is bound to be cheaper to buy, but cloths are among the easiest and quickest kinds of covering you can make yourself and have the advantage that they can be tailor-made to fit an awkwardly shaped room. Before embarking on a large-scale cloth, however, bear in mind that you will need the space to store it flat during the several days it takes to make.

To create your own floorcloth, you will need a piece of tightly woven heavy-weight canvas around 4–5cm (1¾–2in) larger all round than the finished size you are aiming for. Start by tacking or stapling the canvas to a wooden frame made of timber battens, to a board or to the floor. Make a mixture of acrylic primer or emulsion (latex) paint and PVA glue in the proportion of one part PVA to five parts water and apply at least two coats to the underside and a further four or so coats to the top side, until you have built up a smooth surface with as little as possible of the weave still showing. Sand lightly between coats. When dry, remove the cloth from the stretcher, turn under the edges to the exact dimensions you require, mitre the corners and stick down on the underside with PVA.

Paint a base coat in the background colour you have chosen, using flat oil-based paint, then add the design in artist's acrylic or even slightly thinned artist's oil paints. Finally, seal with four or more coats of acrylic or oil-based polyurethane varnish, thinning each coat progressively from a first coat of one part solvent to three parts varnish to a final coat of one to five, again with two coats on the back. The cloth should then be left to dry for at least 24 hours, preferably 48, before laying in place.

The range of patterns and colours you can use is limitless. At one time, cottagers were recommended to select marbled or grained designs that looked like stone or wood, while more prosperous householders could buy floorcloths that imitated carpet. Today, you might consider creating geometric patterns to suit your own interior scheme, whether simple and subtle or bold and bright.

In this otherwise simply furnished room, a bold painted floorcloth stands out from the soft grey floorboards, yet in colours muted enough not to overpower the space. The stylized sunburst design on the floorcloth is an elegant accompaniment to the gracious curves of the wooden sofa. A distressd finish to the painting of both the sofa frame and the skirting underlines the traditional effect.

153

Laying & Maintaining Sheet Flooring

Since they are comparatively light and flexible, sheet materials particularly in tile form are among the easier kinds of flooring to lay yourself and general instructions for this are given on pages 179–80. There are, however, a few points worth bearing in mind when it comes to dealing with specific materials.

Cork tiles supplied with an adhesive backing are extremely easy to lay but will lift at the slightest sign of damp and should therefore be avoided in damp areas. In its natural state cork is a highly absorbent material and unsealed tiles will need to be given at least three coats of protective varnish after laying, or four in areas of heavy traffic or wet use. It may also be worth adding a final coat of sealer to presealed tiles laid in kitchens to minimize patchy wear. Make sure that the surface is completely free of dust and grease before sealing by wiping with a clean white cloth which has been moistened with white spirit.

While all forms of sheet flooring are relatively easy to maintain, regular cleaning is important so that abrasion by grit and dirt does not impair their appearance or damage the seal. Most surfaces can simply be mopped down to remove surface dirt. For sheet, as for stone and ceramic floors, it is worth using soapless detergents. These cleaning agents are based on synthetic chemicals and are particularly valuable in hard water areas, where soaps tend to create scum and leave residual deposits on the surface.

Rubber floors can be polished with a metallized emulsion polish to produce a glossier surface that will better withstand scuffing, but make sure that you follow the manufacturer's recommendations. If the polish begins to wear away, you should remove it all with a proprietary polish remover approved by the manufacturer before reapplying a new coat.

Linoleum can also be given two coats of emulsion polish after washing to seal the surface and then burnished with a soft pad to give it a tougher protective film. Burnishing should remove scuff marks, but if stubborn spots remain, they can be removed by gentle rubbing with wire wool. If the floor becomes very soiled over time, clean off the polish with a water-based polish stripper. Never use solvent-based materials on linoleum.

While sealed cork is impervious to water, it will stain and soil easily if the seal layer breaks down and any marks will be difficult to remove. To prevent staining and to ensure that joints are well sealed, you may need to remove the seal layer after a time, lightly sand the surface and reseal. Special seal removers are available for this purpose. In areas of normal use cork should not need resealing for up to ten years, but in kitchens this period is likely to be around five or six years.

Classic industrial rubber-studded tiles are an essential ingredient in creating this informal high-tech look, along with the exposed steel ceiling beams and exposed metal plumbing. The pale grey of the floor reflects the daylight entering from the large circular skylights to infuse the space with a cool light.

NEW & UNUSUAL FLOORS

The choice of materials used for flooring has always reflected either what is available locally or what has been developed through experiment and innovation. In old charnel houses, for example, the floors were sometimes made from the bones that had been deposited there; while the rubber sheeting and glass floors now common in industrial buildings were first seen in the pioneering Maison de Verre designed by French architect Pierre Chareau in the 1920s. If you are looking for unusual floors that will give your interiors a unique character, it is worth considering some of the flooring products used in commercial, industrial or other non-domestic interiors, where designers have different problems to solve. This is especially true of shop design, since the aim is to make the environment eye-catching to potential customers; and some of the most innovative ideas may be put into practice for that purpose.

Glass is one of the more interesting flooring materials that have made their way from industrial contexts into the home. Initially, thick glass blocks were laid into concrete in pavements to let light into basement rooms. Now glass blocks have become an accepted part of the same industrial high-tech look for interior spaces which includes the use of rubber-sheet and metal-grid flooring. More adventurous still would be to use a material not normally associated with floors, such as leather. For this you will almost certainly have to sacrifice one or more of the normal requirements for flooring – be it durability, longevity or ease of maintenance. Some materials are perfectly suitable for flooring but may not be used because the material or the skills needed to lay it are not easily come by.

Dispensing with some of the practicalities allows great scope for the imagination. For example, a sculptor has created a three-dimensional floor of shaped plywood. Its wavelike forms are not easy to walk on but lend the room a most intriguing quality. Materials such as slatted timber or plastic duckboards designed for wet environments, or bamboo as used on Japanese terraces, or even rope pinned to a timber base in coils or stripes, can all be visually exciting but are usable only if you accept the need to wear strong, flat shoes.

This highly polished floor was created by sanding the cement screed smooth and then applying three coats of acrylic resin. It is sufficiently hard-wearing and cleanable for this artist's studio, yet elegant when the room becomes a living room. The high polish not only reflects light but gives a sophisticated glossiness.

Concrete

Concrete is by no means a new material, and many industrial or utilitarian spaces have long been left with their rough structural concrete slab as a floor. However, people have recently realized that, if laid with care, concrete can be used as a high-quality interior floor, giving a tough but elegant finish not much different in feel from some types of stone. To achieve a simple, acceptably smooth and level surface, the wet concrete is vibrated during construction with a special vibrator which brings the finest particles to the surface and allows the whole to settle very evenly. To obtain an even smoother finish, the concrete can be polished with a machine not unlike that used to polish terrazzo (see page 42), but such work needs to be done by a specialist.

Another alternative is to alter the texture and colour of the concrete. When dry it can be bush-hammered, scored or imprinted with patterns. Or you can insert ceramic tiles or even broken pieces of tile in it to make abstract mosaic-like patterns similar to those pioneered by the Spanish architect Gaudi. Once dry, concrete may be sandblasted into a pattern or simply painted. You can also change concrete by including aggregates or colouring in the concrete mix. One interesting treatment is to lay it smooth; then, when it is almost but not quite dry, treat the surface with a retarding agent. This will inhibit the setting process, allowing you to brush away the fine cement and sand and reveal the rough stone aggregate which is part of all concrete mixes. By applying the retarding agent in limited areas – ideally by using stencils – you can create patterns that exploit the contrast of texture between the treated and the untreated areas. The potential complexity of the pattern is limited only by the amount of work you are prepared to put into it. The resulting hard and very durable floor is ideal for ground-floor bathrooms or utility areas. When considering any of these processes, it is imperative to discuss them beforehand with an engineer or builder, to ensure that you do not weaken the concrete.

Concrete paving slabs can be used in exactly the same way as stone slabs and are very similar as regards temperature and noise. They are available in a range of colours – either greys and buffs or muted reds, greens, yellows and blues. They usually come in 30cm (around 1ft), 45cm (18in) or 60cm (around 2ft) squares, or in 60×30cm (2×1ft) rectangles. Hexagons and circles are also available. With concrete paving slabs you have three style possibilities. First are the plain, flat, machine-pressed slabs which give a completely neutral but tough and practical surface. When polished but left bare or painted or stained with classical patterns such as key squares, they can lend a strong and convincing feel to entrance halls or similar heavy-wear areas – even those with a period character. Second are slabs with rough, textured finishes which attempt to imitate stone, though not always very successfully. Third are coloured slabs which, when used indoors, make a less showy but flat alternative to coloured stone or terracotta. One interesting use of coloured concrete slabs is to inset them into areas of plain poured concrete in either a pattern or random scatter.

All concrete provides a practical surface for utilitarian areas of the house or even for hallways and kitchens. However, concrete, like some stones, does stain, and it generates fine dust. So if you intend to leave it undecorated you should use commercially available sealers which are clear.

ABOVE *This use of polished concrete is bold and three-dimensional. It is cast in situ in such a way that each poured area is designed as a sculptural element – the stairs and lower floor flowing into one. The joint between walls and floor is carefully emphasized by a shadow gap so that the walls appear to float as planes of colour.*

OPPOSITE *Polished concrete paving slabs in this modern house are used in the same way that one might use stone flags, but have an appropriately down-played quality very different from the message that stone would convey. They serve as a tough, uncompromising, economic and neutral floor to offset the sculptural wall forms.*

Metal

Floors made of open grids or plates of steel or aluminium have been used in industrial contexts since steel plate was developed in the nineteenth century. Grids and plate come in many patterns and sizes, but their suitability for flooring in the majority of domestic settings is limited since they are cold and noisy, uncomfortable for children and some can be difficult to clean. You would normally choose such a floor only if you wanted an industrial, high-tech feel. Thick steel plate is very heavy, so open-grid steel or aluminium is usually preferred, especially where a non-slip area is called for, as on a landing or access area, for example. Sheet steel for covering structural floors can be thin – from 1mm (under ¹⁄₁₆in) upwards. The choice of thickness depends on the structural support system on which it is to be laid. As with glass, structural steel requires specialist design and installation.

Thin sheets of steel, zinc, copper or aluminium can be nailed or stuck down to timber. You can also obtain sheet-metal tiles that can be glued down to an existing floor. These consist of a plywood or timber core 12mm (½in) or 19mm (¾in) thick, wrapped in steel or any one of the thin sheet alloys. They are made to order in sizes from 15cm (6in) square up to squares of 1.2m (4ft).

BELOW LEFT *The whole of this interior is crisp, shiny and contemporary, from the glass table and steel columns to the plain bold colours and the metal furniture. The regular grid of steel sheet on the floor adds the finishing touch to this modern style. The shiny reflectivity and the regularity of the grid enhance the overall machine-like effect.*

OPPOSITE *Different patterns of aluminium sheet would suit different qualities of space – the larger diamond shapes conveying a more industrial feel. Mild steel sheet is also available in some of these patterns and is often known as 'chequerplate'.* CLOCKWISE FROM TOP LEFT *tread grip anodized finish; decorative embossed finish; tread grip mill finish; tread grip satinized finish; tread grip bright finish; satin fine line embossed finish.*

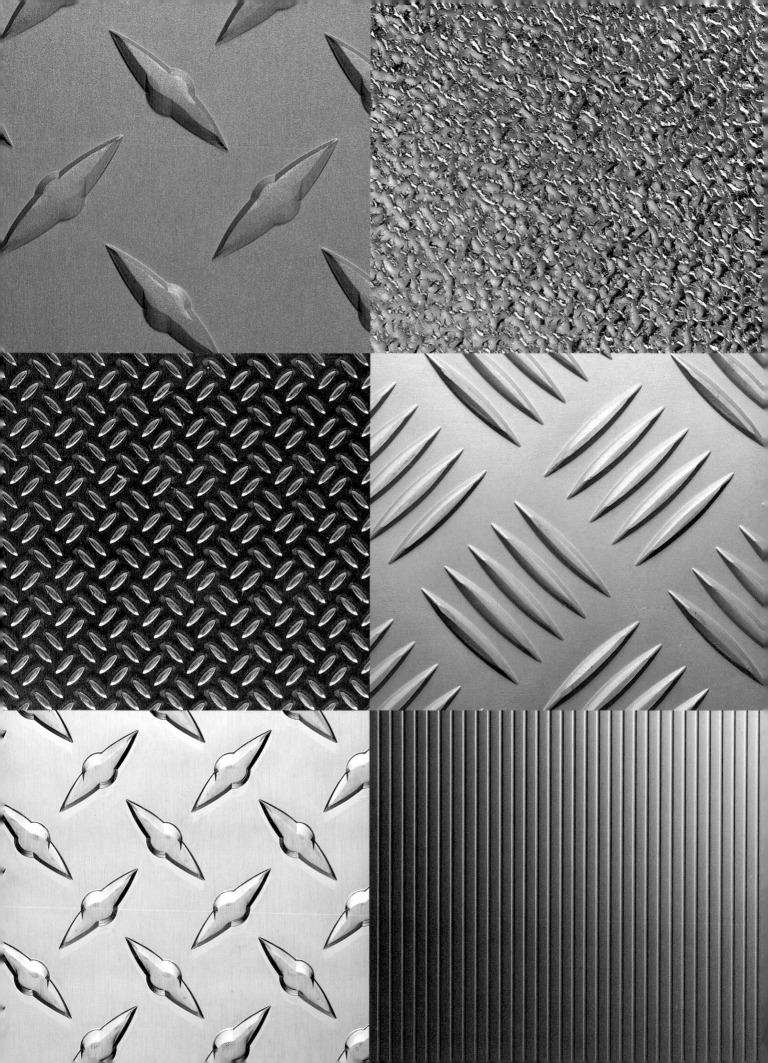

OPPOSITE *This old timber staircase is covered with zinc sheet. Because the zinc can be cut to shape and bent over the front edge of the treads with tin-cutting tools, the effect is that of a metal carpet, in which the regular edge nailing makes a bold visual statement. This stair covering will never wear out and serves as a strong and durable way of reinforcing weak or split stair treads.*

BELOW *The treads of this staircase are made from frosted glass. Not only do they let light filter down to the floor below but, as they are held on brackets away from the walls, they seem to float free in space – an attempt almost to deny the solidity of the stairs.*

Glass

Glass blocks may be set in a honeycomb-like framework of concrete to give a tough 'brutalist' feel and have the advantage of letting light through – useful if you have a badly lit room with a lighter space above. However, glass in floors is essentially a structural rather than a finish material and is generally incorporated by a builder during building or alteration works. It is not something to be installed by an amateur. Thick sheets of glass in steel frames are another alternative for a glass structural floor. These will be less muscular, but still have a modern, rather severe feel. They are frequently used as treads and landings on stairways. Here, very thick, toughened glass must be used, sometimes as thick as 5cm (2in) depending upon the size of the sheets and the spacing of the support beams. Once again, both the glass and its support structure will have to be designed and installed by a specialist.

One disadvantage of glass is that it tends to be slippery and needs a great deal of cleaning. In time it will get scratched, which is why clear glass is seldom used for floors. Instead a milky, opaque glass is chosen – this finish is achieved by etching with acid or sandblasting.

RIGHT *Many elements of high-tech style are present in this one floor: the stainless steel grid as well as the bright-red steel structural beams. These beams hold up the precast sections of concrete, into which circular glass lenses have been set. Each part of the space is made distinct by a different type of floor, the glass and concrete defining the bed area, the timber duckboards and steel plate marking the extent of circulation and other zones.*

LEFT *Glass blocks are set into a concrete grid as a main structural element in the building, and let light down from the overhead skylights into the space below. Lighting from underneath at night gives a warm glow to offset any feeling of coldness normally associated with glass and throws the simple lines of the furniture into sharp silhouette. These glass blocks have a definite 1930s feel.*

Specialist Paints, Leather & Others

Industrial interiors, workshops, factories and similar areas which are subject to heavy wear cannot be floored satisfactorily with normal or even office-standard coverings. A range of extra-tough liquid coatings has been developed for them. Being thixotropic – in other words able to level out cracks or other unevennesses – these coatings are useful for any irregular floor surface. They are therefore ideal not only for use on concrete but also on timber floors where they can mask poor surfaces.

Many different types of paint have been developed for industrial environments, but essentially they are either rubber-based, epoxy-based or polyurethane. Polyurethane paint is the most rigid and will crack if the substrate moves. On boards, therefore, it would be best to use an epoxy-based paint. The most serviceable are epoxy/polyurethane paints which combine the strength and hard-wearing character of polyurethane with the flexibility of epoxy. Rubber paint is also flexible.

Many of these paints demand some skill in application. They also usually require the floor to be thoroughly dry before you start. Most contain a large amount of toxic solvents, so you should wear a protective mask when applying them and ensure the room is very well ventilated. Wherever possible, select a paint with the lowest possible solvent content. The chemical nature of epoxy and polyurethane coatings means that they can react adversely with any substances already on an existing floor, and it is therefore crucial that you use them strictly according to the manufacturers' instructions.

These paints are hard-wearing, practical and easy-to-clean, but are much more expensive than ordinary domestic floor paints. They come in only a limited range of colours, but they do allow you to treat your floor like a giant canvas, painting them on in bold, attractive and unique designs. You also have a choice of a smooth, glossy finish which would suit a modern, high-tech interior, or a matt, slightly stippled finish, more appropriate for areas that may get wet. When applying the paints, make sure that the colours do not bleed into one another. Do this either by stencilling them on, or by using flexible strips of hardboard or thin plastic to outline the areas of different colour and then you can pour or trowel the colours into the separate shapes.

Other unusual 'one-off' floors can be made of salvaged materials not necessarily associated with building. To take one example, old copper printing plates nailed to boards with large studded nails have been used to make a varied and textured floor of endless fascination that looks both contemporary and antique. Salvaged mechanical parts or broken pieces of ceramic can be set in clear resin to make a unique floor mosaic.

Leather has also been used and is relatively soft and warm, deadens sound, can be cleaned and will certainly feel luxurious. It can also be coloured or embossed to provide a patterned surface. You will have to go a long way to find a leather worker to make a floor, but they do exist.

In theory, almost any material that can be laid flat could be used as a floor covering, depending on the amount of wear it is likely to get. If you give free rein to the imagination – and can locate the specialist workers you need – you may well be able to create something entirely out of the ordinary.

OPPOSITE *The designer has used the floor with the freedom of a large canvas to create these striking Miro-like forms using brightly coloured epoxy resin paints. These resin paints are generally thixotropic and can be applied by pouring, which gives the attractive free-form edges.*

ABOVE *This opulent and unique leather floor is in the same vein as the leopard chair. The skins' natural colouring has been left and some of the pieces are almost complete hides which, with their organic shape and stitches along the cut edges, show a clear design theme.*

TECHNIQUES

This chapter covers many practical aspects of laying a range of flooring and includes advice on repairing existing structural floors, which must be in good condition before they are covered. While some of the techniques described can be carried out by home-owners themselves, others are best left to professionals and are outlined here to give an idea of what is involved.

Repairing Timber Floors

Damage to wooden floors is most likely to occur when boards are taken up to install pipes or wiring. Badly split or damaged boards should be replaced, preferably with the longest possible boards, but at any rate with lengths no shorter than the span across three joist spaces (bearing on four joists). This will avoid rocking. Always stagger the joints. If the end of an otherwise good board is split, turn it around so that the split end is under the skirting. Where nail holes have become enlarged replace with screws through the same holes – fixing a nail in another position is likely to cause a split, or you may nail into cables or pipes. Cut nails rather than round wire nails reduce the likelihood of split ends. Where boards have been cut alongside a joist so that one end is not supported, the best practice is to lift the longer board, trim it so that it bears on half of the joist width, and replace the shorter section so it bears fully on the joist. Alternatively screw – do not nail a block of wood to the side of the joist to form a bearing. Newer buildings may have tongued and grooved boards. To remove these you need to saw along the edge of the board to cut through the tongue. This requires some skill and should only be attempted with a floor-board saw, or preferably with a circular saw on which the blade is set to only just less than the board thickness. When repairing a floor, mark the position of any hidden cables and pipes under the boards and behind skirtings.

Finding replacement boards that are the same thickness as old ones can be a problem. It is not advisable to pack up the joists to allow use of thinner boards as the packing usually works loose. Wood yards are used to planing boards down to match existing ones if you provide a sample. Gaps in floorboards can be filled either by the insertion of thin slivers of wood, which need to be glued in place (a procedure requiring considerable skill), or by trowelling one of the proprietary brands of flexible wood fillers into the joint. These come in a range of colours to match different woods. Noisy floors are usually a result of moving boards and can generally be cured by replacing nails with screws in the vicinity of the squeak. Dusting with talcum powder also helps over a limited period.

When you are restoring a floor, try to take into account the age and style of the building. In this old house the boards have been repaired but left rough and unvarnished, which seems appropriate to the crumbling grandeur of the room.

Preparing the Timber Floor Surface

If you have carried out extensive repairs on an old floor which you wish to sand and seal, it is often wise to stain the whole surface before sealing so as to blend in the new boards with the old.

Ensuring that a timber floor is sufficiently level to be covered by other materials can be problematic, and it is often simplest to lay sheets of hardboard (Masonite) or 6mm (¼in) plywood on top of the boards once you have fixed loose boards. Many floor-laying firms will install this underlayer before laying their sheet or carpet. If you decide to do the work yourself, leave the sheets in the heated room for a minimum of 48 hours to acclimatize before fixing. Hardboard is the easier to lay, and should be pinned down with hardboard nails at 150mm (6in) intervals. Use 6mm (¼in) plywood on very uneven floors, and screw down at similar intervals. If you plan to lay ceramic or stone onto a boarded timber floor you will need to use 12mm (½in) WBP grade plywood (moisture-resistant) board and seal the underside and all the edges with a varnish to prevent moisture ingress which could destroy tile adhesion. When laying all such boards, leave 1mm (¹⁄₁₆in) gaps all round each sheet to allow expansion, and 3mm (⅛in) at the edges of the room. Allow access to services by cutting strips of sheet to coincide with boards that run over pipes and cables, and screwing them down rather than using nails, so they can be easily lifted.

Dealing with Damp in Timber Floors

Rot in timber floors is most likely to be caused by damp and needs to be addressed before laying any new flooring. It may be that timbers are in contact with damp earth or with other damp parts of the building structure, or there may be a slowly leaking hidden pipe or seepage from a shower or bath. There is no point in replacing affected timber without dealing with the cause. If the timber floor is very springy, the timber beams or joists may be undersized, in which case the only solution is a major reconstruction. But it is also possible that the ends of joists set into an outside wall have been softened by damp rot. Any such signs are best investigated by an independent architect, building surveyor or one of the many specialist firms who will carry out a survey and give you a quotation without charge. The reputable firms can generally be relied upon to give an accurate report, but it is always advisable to obtain two survey quotes.

Repairing Concrete Floors

Concrete floors are usually covered with a sand and cement screed varying in thickness from 4cm to 6cm (1½ to 2½in), which creates a smooth and level finish. If you plan to lay a stone or ceramic floor using the sand and cement method (see page 178), this will iron out minor problems in screed finishes, but for carpet, and particularly sheet coverings, careful repair of cracks and other damage is necessary. Before carrying out any work ascertain whether there are any cables or pipes buried within the concrete, which is often the case. Pipes rising out of the floor nearby will suggest a pipe run within the screed, and socket outlets in walls or skirtings indicate that there may be an electrical cable in the floor. If carrying out extensive work, use a wire sensor, obtainable from DIY stores or consult an electrician. Tap the floor with a hard object – any change from a dull thud to a hollow sound will reveal a loss of adhesion to the structural slab below. Small areas of loss – about the size of a dinner plate – are unlikely to present a problem. A crumbling screed might mean that the original mix was faulty and the whole surface needs stabilizing or even renewing. If you are doing the repairs yourself, cut back to where the screed firmly adheres, preferably with an undercut. Cracks smaller than about 3 or 4mm (around ⅛in) can be ignored, provided there is no crumbling or lack of key, but larger gaps should be cut out to a width of about 2cm (¾in). Once the damaged screed has been removed, ensure surfaces are entirely free from all dust or loose particles and coat the base and sides of the hole with a thin coating of PVA general purpose builders' adhesive, following the manufacturer's recommendations for dilution. Trowel firmly into all crevices a mix consisting of one part cement to three parts sand mixed with water and PVA in equal amounts, which should be wetter than damp, but not running wet. Drying time will depend on the thickness of the screed, and may take a week or more. Do not try to accelerate the process with heat, as the repair will crack. If the top layer of a screed is sandy or dusty it can be sealed with PVA or a proprietary sealer to prevent crumbling.

Uneven screeds will normally be levelled by the floor layers. If they do not do this, they should confirm prior to laying that the floor is adequate. As sand and cement screeds will crack when thinner than about 3cm (1¼in), any levelling or filling of screeds is done with epoxy or latex levelling compounds, which can be feathered down to as little as 2mm (less than ⅛in).

damaged area of screed

screed

concrete

ABOVE: REPAIRING A SCREED AND CONCRETE FLOOR *A patch of cement and sand screed is repaired by cutting back to where an existing screed is sound and finishing the edge with an undercut, coating the edges and base with PVA adhesive, and trowelling in the new 1/3 cement/sand mix.*

Dealing with Damp in Concrete Floors

Wherever possible, you should try to eliminate damp as it will cause deterioration of floor coverings and other elements of the structure and will adversely affect most adhesives. A damp screed usually indicates either that there has been a failure of the damp-proof membrane (a layer of polythene or bitumen laid by the builder and designed specifically to keep out ground damp) or that water is seeping in, probably from a buried pipe. In such cases, cut out the affected screed, either repair the pipe or repaint the damp-proof membrane on the concrete and replace the screed, as described above. Damp can also penetrate a floor where the edges touch an outside wall, in which case it may be necessary for a builder to install a damp-proof course vertically to isolate the edge of the floor from the wall.

If there is dampness throughout the whole floor there is probably no damp-proof membrane at all, and the only solution is to paint on one of the many bituminous or silicone-based damp-proofing liquids before laying any new floor. Maximum acceptable dampness figures for different floor materials are quoted by the manufacturers, and you should ensure that the floor layer confirms that your floors meet the manufacturer's requirements.

In some cases it may not be possible to cure damp, particularly in thick-walled old stone houses, but there are still a few options available. You could paint a new damp-proof membrane onto the old screed and then lay a stone or ceramic floor on top using the thick-bed method (see page 176); or lay a floating timber floor on polythene damp-proof sheet; or use one of the rubber or vinyl floors that do not need gluing. Claims made for the damp-proofing properties of a number of rubber carpet underlays, chemical epoxy or polyurethane paints and adhesives must be treated with caution.

Insulating Ground Floors

If you intend to leave an existing ground-level timber floor uncovered, particularly if you will be sanding the boards, it is worthwhile insulating it first with mineral wool or one of the semi-rigid insulation bats, preferably 75 or 150mm (3 or 6 in) thick. The boards must first be lifted. Although this is a relatively straightforward task, it does require patience, care and some skill and should ideally be undertaken by a carpenter. To hold the insulating material in place under the boards, garden netting or wire mesh is then laid over the entire floor area sufficiently loosely so that it drops below the joists by the thickness of the material. It is important that the space between the suspended floor and the earth below is well ventilated to prevent damp and rot in the timbers: make sure that air bricks are never blocked.

Solid ground floors can be insulated by laying 25 or 40mm (1 or 1½in) of rigid polystyrene or polyurethane slab onto the concrete and covering this with tongued and grooved sheets of 19mm (¾in) plywood or flooring grade chipboard. Alternatively, you can form a timber boarded floor of 19mm (¾in) boards on 25 or 40mm (1 or 1½in) battens, spaced 40cm (16in) apart, and lay insulation quilt between the battens before fixing down the boards. If you decide to lay such floor, remember that the height of doors, skirtings and other fittings will have to be adjusted to accommodate the extra thickness.

BELOW: INSULATING TIMBER GROUND FLOORS
Existing boards are removed and a mesh is loosely laid over the joists to support mineral wool insulation between the joists. Insulation should not be less than 75mm (3in) and preferably up to 150mm (6in).

FAR BELOW: INSULATING SOLID GROUND FLOORS *Timber battens are laid onto a solid ground floor to support a new timber overlay floor. The space between the battens is filled with insulation and can also be a route for pipes. The battens should be either 40 or 60cm (16 or 24in) apart, depending on the floor thickness (19 or 22mm - just under or just over ¾in respectively). The height of the battens can vary to accommodate more insulation.*

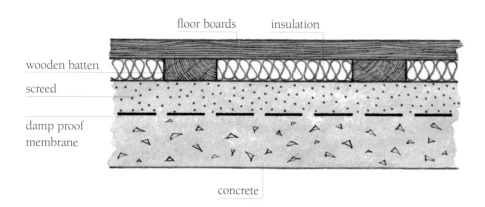

floor boards

joist

insulation quilt held by supporting mesh

floor boards   insulation

wooden batten

screed

damp proof membrane

concrete

Floating Floors & Sound Insulation

Noise consists of either impact sound or airborne sound, and each requires a different method of treatment. Impact sound is usually problematic where footfalls are transmitted to the floor below. Carpet or cushion-backed vinyl can prevent this, but if you want a hard surface you will need to lay a floating floor.

There are a number of types of floating floor, but the principle is always the same: a resilient layer isolates your hard floor surface from the structural floor and the two must not be connected by fixings – hence the term 'floating'. Timber overlay floors are the easiest, as they are designed to lie loose over structural floors, and a resilient layer, usually made of mineral wool or cork between 6 and 12mm (¼ and ½in) thick can be introduced between the two – the thicker the better. Alternatively you can form a floating floor of plywood, chipboard sheet or timber boards resting on rubber-backed battens laid on the structural floor at 40cm (16in) centres for 19mm (¾in) board or 60cm (2ft) centres for 22mm (⅞in) board. The battens are not fixed down, but when the floorboards or sheet are nailed to them they will not move. Specialist sound-reducing systems which combine chipboard or plywood bonded with resilient layers are available for either overlay or structural floors. This kind of floor will be necessary in apartment buildings.

Airborne sound needs to be dealt with in two ways: it has to be prevented from going through the structure, which can only be done by heavy construction, and it needs to be prevented from reverberating round the room, which can only be done by absorbing it with soft materials. Airborne sound travels upwards as well as down, and you may need to insulate a child's bedroom located over a living room as much as a living room over a bedroom or study. Filling the void between the ceiling and floorboards with sound-reducing quilt or sometimes even sand is one of the few ways of reducing the travel of airborne sound between rooms. However, while quilt absorbs

BELOW: FLOATING FLOOR *Sheets of tongued and grooved ply or chipboard are laid over a rigid resilient layer laid onto the existing floor. This is an alternative to using battens, as below. This method can be used on concrete floors and is also effective for thermal insulation.*

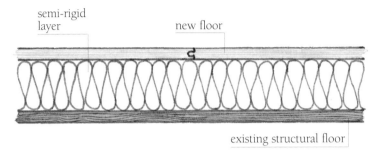

semi-rigid layer   new floor

existing structural floor

BELOW: FLOATING FLOOR WITH BATTENS *Overlay boards are laid on battens which are isolated from the structural floor by resilient rubber or foam pads to prevent transmission of impact sound. Airborne sound is reduced by the absorbent quilt filling the space between boards and concrete floor.*

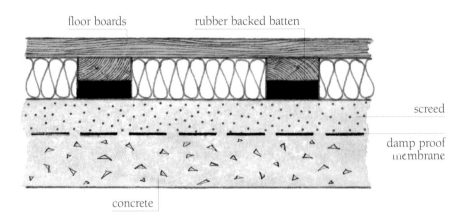

floor boards   rubber backed batten

screed

damp proof membrane

concrete

BELOW: SOUND INSULATION IN EXISTING OR NEW TIMBER FLOORS *The void between the floorboards and the ceiling can be filled with sound-absorbing quilt to reduce transmission of airborne sound. Alternatively, increase the mass of the floor by adding a layer of sand, but first check that the floor structure is able to support the extra weight.*

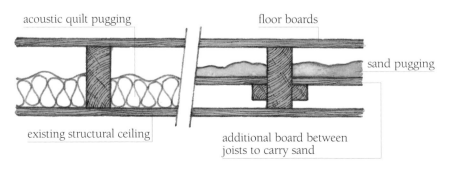

acoustic quilt pugging   floor boards

sand pugging

existing structural ceiling   additional board between joists to carry sand

high-frequency sound, the bass of a stereo can only be stopped from travelling between spaces by mass. The proprietary overlay sound-reduction systems are designed for different ranges of noise. A tiled or stone floor will add considerable extra mass in itself and may solve the problem but will also tend to create a hard echoing space in which noise is bounced from surface to surface. In that case the only solution is to provide soft furnishings, rugs or carpet.

Underfloor Heating

The Romans heated their floors in cold Northern Europe with underground hot-air ducts, and today improvements in materials and an understanding of building performance are making underfloor heating popular. The heat is at low level, where it is needed; it counteracts draughts; it is an ideal way of taking the cold out of stone and tile floors; and it avoids the difficulty of siting radiators. As fluctuations in temperature adversely affect old buildings, it is also a sensible way of heating traditional houses. The principle is that, since the floor is such a large area, the whole of its surface acts as a heat source, requiring only a small difference in surface temperature to heat the space. With solid concrete floors, which store heat, only a small amount of heat is fed into the floor. Underfloor heating can be equally successful with sheet materials and can also be used under timber floors, though particular care must be taken to ensure that the appropriate timbers are used to avoid cracking and that the system is properly designed and installed. Timber floors do not act as a heat store and additional insulation under the floor will be needed to prevent the heat from seeping downwards.

The heat source for underfloor heating can be either electrical (in which case cheap-rate night-time supplies can be used) or through long joint-free coils connected to the hot-water pipes of a normal central-heating boiler. The screeds into which these are laid must be at least 10cm (4in) thick. Alternatively, thin fabric-like mats incorporating electric heating coils can be laid within thick-bed adhesives for stone and ceramic floors, avoiding the need for a new screed in an existing construction, but these are designed not so much to heat the space as to take off the chill. Specifying the correct construction and installation for underfloor heating is a skilled technical matter and should be done by specialists.

BELOW: UNDERFLOOR HEATING IN A NEW CONSTRUCTION *Electric heating coils or hot-water pipes are laid onto the concrete slab which has insulation placed underneath it so that the slab can act as a heat store.*

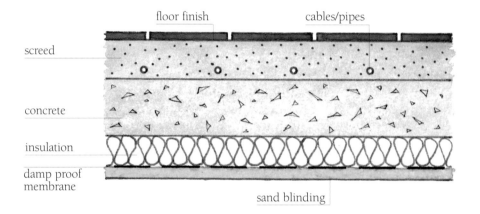

ABOVE: UNDERFLOOR HEATING IN AN EXISTING CONSTRUCTION *Rigid purpose-made insulation is laid onto the existing slab and a thick screed, which must be reinforced with wire mesh, contains the electric cable or hot-water pipes.*

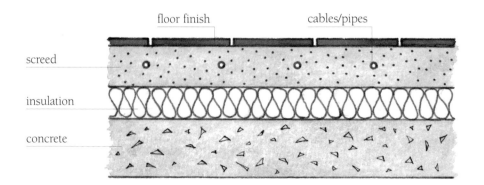

Doormats & Matwells

Doormats are important in keeping floors looking good since they trap not only the visible dirt but those tiny pieces of grit which are so destructive to all finishes. Doormats of the traditional size – around 45×60cm (18×24in) – are relatively ineffective: a mat about 2m (6ft 6in) long is ideal, allowing at least two steps to rid shoes of outside debris. Where there is not enough space for such a large mat, it is therefore useful to have a weatherproof ridged rubber or metal scraper outside, as well as a mat inside the door. A wide range of mats is available: coir in traditional natural brown, and various plain colours and patterns; ridged coir strips alternating with steel or wire; ridged nylon mats – both with and without aluminium strips – in a variety of dirt-masking colours; ridged rubber mats; mats with rows of stiff plastic bristles rather like large toothbrushes; and thin cotton mats. Cotton has the significant advantage of being the most absorbent and washable, and if used inside with an external scraper mat will take the maximum amount off the underside of shoes. These different mats are available in premade sizes or can be cut to fit a matwell. In order to be effective, mats should be kept clean, but this can be difficult. Shake or beat your mat outside, or vacuum clean it. However, there is little that can be done to clean a very soiled coir mat.

To avoid the danger of tripping, you should ideally recess thick mats in a matwell so that they sit flush with the floor. This is something to remember when constructing a new floor. It is possible to form matwells in most existing timber floors by trimming the floor joists so as to lower the boards. Re-use the boards to make a mitred frame around the matwell to create a finished look. Forming a matwell on solid floors is simple if there is a screed, which can

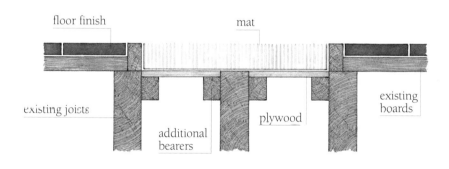

be cut away using a bolster chisel. Screw a timber or metal matwell frame onto the concrete base and fill any rough edge between the screed and the back of the frame with a mortar mix as described for repairing concrete floors on page 170–1. Any damage to a damp-proof membrane should be repaired before covering it with a levelling compound. It is best to take the mat right across your space to the skirting – this will not only give you a larger mat but look more finished and make floor cleaning simpler.

You might find that stone, tiles or carpet are sufficiently thick to accommodate a mat without needing a recessed well. A timber edge looks good between mat and carpet. With stone a thin brass matwell edge may be most suitable as it will hardly be visible. Even with a doormat, you may wish to protect particularly fine carpet near external doors by throwing down a section of natural fibre carpet bound as a mat in the worst weather. Remember that certain bituminous or rubber-backed mats will cause discoloration to some vinyl floors – check with the flooring manufacturer.

ABOVE: RECESSED MATWELL IN AN EXISTING TIMBER JOISTED FLOOR *The boards are replaced by new plywood laid flush with the joists and supported on bearers, which must be securely screwed to the joists. A timber frame is made to trim the floor finish. This will be the thickness of the existing boards plus that of the new floor finish. For greater depth it is also possible to trim the joist and lower the support, but this should only be done after establishing that the strength of the joists is adequate.*

Laying Ceramic Tiles & Stone Flags

Stone or ceramic tiles are laid by one of three methods, according to their nature and that of the existing floor. Thin-bed adhesive, which is no more than 2–5mm (⅛–¼in) thick, and thick-bed adhesive, which is 5–12mm (¼–½in) thick, are used on timber floors or on concrete where there is limited space or height. A sand and cement bed, which is 25mm (1in) or more thick, is used only on concrete floors. This should deal with any hollows in the floor, otherwise fill in any depressions. If laying tiles on timber floors, cover the boards with 12mm (½in) WBP plywood first to provide an even rigid surface. Providing the floor structure is strong enough, ply can also be used as a base for laying large stone slabs with thick-bed adhesive. It will be worth removing skirtings before you start laying tiles, so that when replaced they will hide any cut edges around the edge of the room. To provide a firm edge against which to

RIGHT: FINDING THE CENTRE POINT *Begin by finding the centre points of one pair of opposite walls and drawing a line across the floor to connect them. Repeat for the other pair. Where the two lines intersect will be the centre point of the room. If the room is not quite square, decide with which wall the tiles are to run parallel and set up a right-angled intersection based on this. In kitchens, you may wish to ensure that tiles are running parallel with a run of units.*

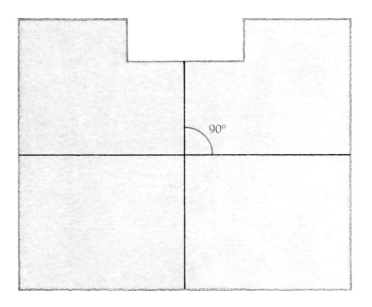

RIGHT: LAYING A 'DRY' RUN *Once you have established the centre point, place one tile in the angle where the two lines intersect and lay loose tiles in single rows from the centre out towards all four walls, following the lines. This will enable you to see if the tiles fit exactly across the room and, if not, what size gaps are left at the walls.*

lay tiles, you can nail a wooden batten across doorways. Bear in mind, too, that a marked increase in the height of the floor may mean removing the door and planing the bottom before rehanging. (This will apply to all kinds of flooring which add any depth to the existing structure.)

Thin-bed adhesives are used for thinner stone and ceramic tiles. These are available ready-mixed or in powder form, and there are waterproof types for wet areas. Use cement-based adhesives on concrete floors and one of the flexible epoxy or rubber-based types on wooden floors. Some adhesives require a primer coat. Manufacturers of adhesives provide comprehensive detailed technical literature which should always be referred to, as well as specialist trowels which are designed to ensure the proper texture and thickness of spread. For cutting tiles to fit round edges, you can hire a professional tile cutter which will deal with most ceramic and thinner quarry tiles. For thicker tiles it is better to use an angle grinder, also available from hire shops, but these are dangerous and

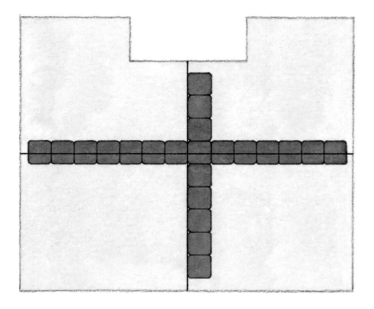

LEFT: REPOSITIONING THE TILES *It is unlikely that the room will accommodate an exact number of tiles without gaps. You will probably need to adjust the position of the tiles so that any spaces between the last whole tile in the row and the wall are even. The aim is to have cut tiles of the same size at opposite walls.*

RIGHT: IRREGULAR ROOMS *Where rooms are irregular in shape, arrange for the tile pattern in the main part of the room to fit as described above. Then lay further dry runs towards odd corners and angles in the walls. If possible, make sure that any cuts required to fit awkward shapes are in unobtrusive places.*

must be used with utmost care. Arrange the work so that there is no need to walk on laid areas for the prescribed period – sometimes as long as four days. If a room needs to be used, lay the floor in two halves. Floors always move, so a gap for movement of 3–5mm (around ⅛–¼in) at the perimeters is essential — if none is advised make enquiries of the material manufacturer.

The sand and cement method is always used for thick stone flags and is also preferable for thicker and uneven hand-made terracotta tiles. Although they can be laid using adhesives, quarry tiles are also often laid on a sand and cement bed. Lay a mixture of three or four parts sand to one part cement to a thickness of no less than 25mm (1in), or possibly 35mm (1½in) in the case of stone. Wet the tile to prevent drying out, coat the back with a slurry of neat cement and tap firmly into place. When using uneven natural slabs it is best to start with the thickest to establish a level. Some manufacturers consider a 10mm (⅜in) bed of sand and cement adequate, but if you only have this amount of space I would recommend using an adhesive instead. In instances where the main structural floor may not be completely dry or stable, such as occurs with new concrete

RIGHT: LAYING TILES DIAGONALLY *Establish the centre point of the room, as shown on page 176. Lay a wooden batten at an angle of 45 degrees to the marking lines. Using the batten as a guide, place a 'dry' run of tiles diagonally across the room. If necessary, shift the tiles to even up the spaces at each end of the run.*

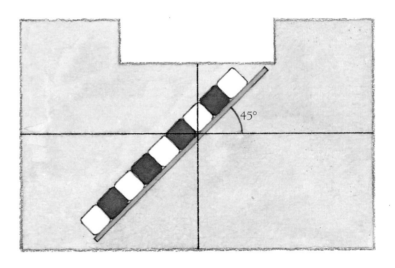

RIGHT: LAYING TILES DIAGONALLY WITH BORDERS *To surround a floor of diagonally laid tiles with a straight border, lay a 'dry' run of tiles along a batten as outlined above. Working from the centre, begin filling one quarter of the room with tiles. The last complete tile nearest the wall gives you a marker for a setting-out line to be drawn parallel to the wall. Lay a dry run of primary border tiles in one quadrant and trim tiles if necessary to fit. Avoid trimming tiles to less than half their width. Infill the secondary border, cutting tiles as necessary to fit against the walls. Repeat for the other three quadrants.*

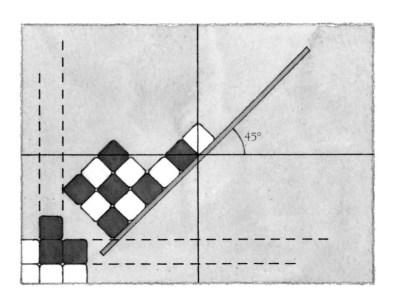

slabs or underfloor heating, some manufacturers advise laying a screed on a separating layer of polythene so that the tiles and the screed will not be affected by structural movement. In this case the screed should be no less than 6cm (2½in) thick and the work needs to be done to a very high standard. This kind of construction is best left to builders.

To achieve the right spacing between tiles, use plastic spacers, matches or other regular spacers, unless the tiles have spacing nibs along the edge. Older floors tended to be laid with much tighter joints, whereas today joints are often as wide as 12mm (½in). This will detract from the quality of the floor – even though some layers recommend thick joints as a feature. Once the tiles are laid and completely dry, trowel grout well into the joints and wipe off all surplus after no more than 10–15 minutes. Unless the tiles are glazed always coat them with an initial layer of the recommended sealer before grouting to avoid staining. Grout is available in different colours, and a flexible grout must be used on a timber floor. Unless you wish to use the lines of the joints as a contrasting pattern, it is important to blend the colour of the grout carefully with the material. The irregular edges of hand-made tiles are one of their characteristic features and should never be 'evened up'. To reveal the edges, set the grout slightly lower, while at the same time avoiding any sharp protruding corners.

Broken tiles cannot be repaired and will have to be replaced. Starting at the centre, use a hammer and cold chisel (or large nail) to crack the unwanted tile into smaller pieces and chip these away from the base, taking care not to damage the edges of the surrounding tiles. Scrape or chip off as much of the remaining bedding and adhesive as possible. Ensure that you make sufficient depth for the replacement tile to sit flush with the surrounding floor, remove all dirt and apply tile adhesive to the tile. If large areas need replacing it is best to replace the base as well as the tiles.

Laying Flexible Sheet Flooring & Tiles

Linoleum, vinyl, rubber and cork are all laid using essentially the same methods, although different adhesives may be recommended by the manufacturers of different materials. Because flexible sheet flooring is comparatively thin, any unevenness in the base will show through and it is worth taking time over preparation to ensure the underlying floor is smooth. Remove concrete floorpaints or previous adhesives. Existing tiles should be removed or, if firmly stuck, cleaned with a cleaner recommended by the adhesive manufacturer.

Before cutting, all materials should be unwrapped and left loose to acclimatize for at least 24 hours in the room at its natural temperature. To lay sheet flooring, start by cutting it to a size about 5cm (2in) larger than the dimensions of the room. Spread it out and, beginning with the longest straight wall, measure to ensure that any pattern is even and runs parallel to this wall. Mark and score the sheet accurately to fit the wall before trimming to the other walls and around fittings. Once the sheet has been cut to size, roll one half back to the middle of the room, apply adhesive to the floor and then carefully roll the sheet back into place, pushing it into the adhesive to avoid trapping any air. Repeat the same process for the other half of the room. Finish by smoothing the whole surface from the centre outwards with a 70kg (150lb) roller (which can be hired) to ensure adhesion and avoid any bubbles. Most sheet flooring is available in widths of 4m (13ft), so joints may not be necessary. If you do need to make a join, a solvent weld can be used, although professional seaming with heat-welded strips is preferable.

To lay flexible tiles, start from the centre so that cuts are confined to the edges, unless you are laying a pattern which requires more cutting, in which case this will need to be marked on the floor first. Find the centre point and establish the extent of symmetry in the room (see page 176). Once you have the main guidelines you can simply butt the tiles against each other. After laying out the tiles 'dry' to see how the whole floor looks, spread the adhesive to the recommended thickness with the trowel provided. You can buy self-adhesive tiles with peel-off backings, but they tend to stay in place less securely and are particularly prone to being affected by the slightest hint of damp. Cut the edge tiles to fit the walls and lay these last. Trimming sheet flooring around shapes such as pipes, radiators and bathroom fittings is most easily done using a profile comb, which allows you to trace the outline onto the material before cutting. It is worth cutting a trial outline in thick card as a final check before cutting the sheet. Ensure that borders are carefully measured and correctly positioned in relation to the walls. Small key square inserts can be laid in any tiles – or even sheet – except cushioned vinyl. These should be cut and laid after the main squares have been laid but before the adhesive dries, and in larger rooms it may be worth fixing the key squares as you complete each quarter section of the room. Cut an accurate card template the size of the small key square and use to mark both the piece to be cut out and the section to be removed, or alternatively cut your key squares and use these as templates for the cut-outs.

An extensive range of adhesives is available for different floor materials and conditions. Rubber resin types are used for some vinyls, linoleum and cork tiles; water-based, solvent-free, acrylic emulsion types for vinyl sheet and tiles; rubber emulsion paste for lino and cork; and two-part solvent-free epoxy for rubber sheet or floors and in areas with moisture. In small areas or with foam-backed vinyl sheet you may only need to use adhesive at the edges, in which case the rubber resin type is suitable. Select an adhesive that remains wet and allows adjustment. The larger manufacturers make a wide range of products including repair compounds, sealers, levellers and adhesives, many of which are solvent-free, and it is essential to ensure that all different components you use are compatible with each other as well as the flooring material. If you have underfloor heating check with manufacturers that adhesives are suitable.

Laying Carpet

Carpet laying is simple in principle, but in practice requires a good degree of skill and is ideally left to the carpet supplier, whose charges may be relatively low. Although it is possible to lay with tape and tacks, the best way of fitting is to use gripper strips which are nailed or glued along the edge of the room 12mm (½in) from the skirting board. The underlay is then cut to butt up to the gripper rod. Carpet should initially be cut some 15cm (6in) larger than the room, depending on the size of the pattern, and laid in place so that the pattern and alignment best suit the room when viewed from the doorway. Starting in one corner, push the carpet into the gripper rods, stretching it to fit with a toothed knee kicker (which can be hired). Getting carpet sufficiently tight so that it does not rise in folds with use is important. The stretching is the difficult but crucial process and once the carpet is in the gripper rods it is virtually impossible to remove it. Lay grippers across doors, and if joining two pieces lay two grippers 10mm (just under ½in) each side of the centre line of the door so that each piece finishes under the door when it is closed. You might want to fix a metal cover strip over this, or preferably lay an adhesive carpet strip underneath the joint and press the two edges together.

On stairs you can hold the carpet in place with gripper rods or with stair rods and brackets – a very traditional and stylish fixing method suitable for older houses. Using stair rods allows you to move the carpet occasionally to minimize wear, but you should allow some extra carpet at the top and bottom if you plan to do this. If you use the more common gripper rod method, attach the gripper rod to the back of each tread and at the bottom of each riser so the two pieces almost abutt. Cut underlay in sections and lay on the treads only, but projecting over, and tuck around and under the nosing before stapling in place. Stair carpet should be laid with the pile direction facing down the stairs. Landing carpet should be taken over the top nosing and down the last riser where it meets the stair carpet.

Carpet tiles are easy to lay, and should be simply butted tightly up to each other with the perimeter tiles cut to a tight fit against the skirting. Adhesive only needs applying at points of pivot such as the top and bottom of stairs, and at the centre tile to avoid movement during laying. Mark the centre out and lay the centre tile first, preferably using peel-off self-adhesive tape. The rest of the tiles will remain in place without needing to be stuck down.

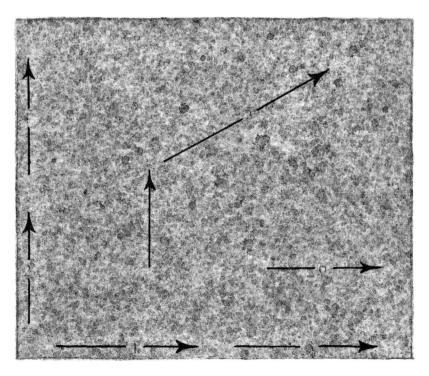

LEFT: LAYING CARPET *It is essential to stretch the carpet tight and this is best done by fixing one corner then working alternately along first the longer (1) and then the shorter wall (2) adjacent to the corner. When the first two walls are complete (3 and 4), stretch the carpet towards the corner diagonally opposite the starting point (5) and continue fixing along the walls towards it (6) As you go, stretch the carpet continuously away from the first fixed long wall and press it firmly home into the gripper with a bolster chisel.*

Removing Stains from Stone

Stones, particularly marbles, can stain if left unsealed. Because deep stains are hard to remove, act quickly to blot up the spill using a plain white cloth. (Do not wipe the spill as this will spread it.) Then rinse the area with water. The key to removing a stain is to identify the substance that caused it. Some stains are washable, but deeper ones may need a poultice, and iron in particular may never be removed entirely. It would be wise to ask the floor supplier to provide you with a small quantity of the appropriate poultice material and keep this to hand. Otherwise you can make your own from the ingredients listed under individual stains below. Spread the poultice about 6mm (¼in) thick over the stain, cover it with a small piece of polythene, and seal the edges with tape. Leave on the affected area for up to 24 hours, then remove the plastic and allow to dry – this may take another 24 hours. It is the drying that draws out the stain. Rinse the area thoroughly with water and buff dry, repeating if necessary. A poultice can also be applied by soaking a gauze pad in the liquid and using it in the same way. Avoid mixing different chemicals, and never mix bleach and ammonia – the resultant gas can be lethal.

OIL-BASED STAINS (grease, tar, cooking oil, milk, cosmetics, oil-based paints) the oil base is likely to darken the stone and must be dissolved so that the stain can be washed out. Cleaning very gently with a soft cloth use only one of these: a liquid cleanser with bleach, household detergent, ammonia or acetone. For poultices mix baking soda and water.
ORGANIC STAINS (coffee, tea, fruit juices, food, urine) these normally cause a pinkish-brown stain. Use a solution of 12% hydrogen peroxide and a few drops of ammonia. For poultices mix kaolin, fuller's earth, powdered chalk or talc with either 12% hydrogen peroxide solution or acetone.
INKS on light stones only, clean with bleach or hydrogen peroxide. On dark stones only, use acetone.
PAINT for oil-based paint, see above. Vinyl, latex or acrylic paints should be scraped off either with a wooden or plastic spatula or very carefully with a razor blade. Large areas of spillage may need paint stripper if scraping does not work; this may etch the stone, and localized repolishing will be needed.
SCRATCHES AND DENTS slight surface damage may be buffed with dry steel wool, or use commercially available marble polishing powder according to the instructions, which usually advise a final buffing with a buffing pad on a low-speed drill.
RUST orange or brown stains, or green if caused by copper or bronze, are difficult to remove and you should probably consult a specialist. Take special care to avoid rust stains by keeping iron furniture or objects away from any water on the floor.

Removing Stains from Carpet

The faster you act when something is spilled on your carpet, the better your chances of preventing a permanent stain. If liquids are spilled, soak up as much as you can with absorbent tissue. Never rub, always blot. Solids, such as greases and tar, should be scraped off with a knife.

GREASE after scraping off any solids, blot up the residue with proprietary dry-cleaning fluid, blotting frequently with an absorbent cloth.
OIL PAINT blot up excess spillage, dab with dilute carpet shampoo on a white cloth, dab with clean water and blot with a dry cloth. When dry, brush the area.
EMULSION PAINT (LATEX) blot up excess spillage, clean the area with cold water and apply diluted carpet shampoo. Follow this with clean water, blot dry and brush.
FRUIT JUICE, COFFEE, TEA, RED WINE, SHERRY moisten a white cloth with diluted carpet shampoo and warm water. Blot up all residual moisture. Brush the affected area in the direction of the pile.
MILK use the same technique as for fruit juice, but apply a proprietary dry-cleaning fluid on the remaining grease.
BLOOD soak up with absorbent tissue and dab the area with a white cloth moistened with cold water.
URINE mop up immediately and dab the area with diluted carpet shampoo and a weak solution of vinegar (1 tablespoon per pint). Blot with absorbent tissue and brush in the direction of the pile.
LIQUID INK after blotting up, rinse with warm water, blotting up as you go. Apply diluted carpet shampoo and dab with clean water.
BALL-POINT INK moisten with clear methylated spirit and dab with clean warm water, before brushing in the direction of the pile.
CHEWING GUM use proprietary freezing agent according to the manufacturer's instructions.

Wood Suitable for Flooring

The following table lists timbers commonly used for floors and generally available. Other timbers are also suitable but less frequently available and have therefore not been included. Among these are silver fir, Western white pine, Spanish or sweet chestnut. Tropical timbers such as mahogany, afrormosia and teak are endangered species and have been omitted. If considering a tropical hardwood for your floor, ensure that it comes from properly managed forests. Always ensure proper moisture content for all timber.

SOFTWOOD	Visual characteristics	Availability	Width of boards	Relative Cost
Douglas fir	orange-brown straight grain	good	wide	medium/high
Larch	orange-red straight grain can be knotty	medium	wide	low/medium
Norway spruce	very pale yellow-brown straight grain	good	wide	low/medium
Red pine (Canadian)	light red-brown straight, indistinct grain fine texture	medium	medium/wide	low/medium
Scots pine (European Redwood)	yellow to red-brown distinct grain can be knotty	good	medium/wide	low/medium
Western hemlock	very pale brown straight grain even texture	good	wide	medium
HARDWOOD				
American cherry	rich reddish brown straight grain fine texture	medium	narrow/medium	medium/high
American red oak	pink-red straight grain coarse texture	good	medium/wide	medium
American walnut	brown to purplish black, pale brown coarse grain even texture	limited	medium	high
American white oak	pale yellow-brown to pale reddish brown straight grain, coarse to medium texture	good	wide	medium/high
Common ash	white/very pale brown straight grain coarse texture	good	medium/wide	medium
Common beech	whitish-pale brown to yellow-brown straight grain fine texture	good	narrow/ medium	medium
English elm	pale brown straight or interlocked grain coarse texture	scarce	medium/wide	high
European oak	yellow to pale brown straight grain coarse texture	good, species may vary	medium/wide	high
European sycamore	yellow/white straight or wavy grain	good	medium/wide	medium/high
Jarrah	red brown straight or wavy grain medium/coarse texture	medium	medium/wide	high
Rock maple	white brown straight grain fine texture	good	medium/wide	medium/high

SOURCES

AKZO NOBEL DECORATIVE COATINGS
Wood stains and paints
PO Box 37, Crown House,
Hollins Road, Darwen BB3 OBG
Tel: 01254 704951

ALTRO FLOORS
Sheet and paint-on finishes
Works Road, Letchworth,
Herts SG6 1NW
Tel: 01462 480480

AMORIM (UK) LTD
Manufacturers of Wicanders flooring:
cork and composite wood flooring suppliers
Amorim House, Star Road, Partridge
Green, Horsham, RH13 8RA
Tel: 01403 710001

THE AMTICO COMPANY LTD
Wide range PVC-faced sheet and tiles
PO Box 42, Kingfield Road,
Coventry CV6 5PL
Tel: 01203 861400

C F ANDERSON AND SON LTD
Timber suppliers
228 London Road, Marks Tey,
Colchester, Essex CO6 1HD
Tel: 01206 211666

THE ANTIQUE TIMBER COMPANY
Reclaimed timber boards and wood blocks
Lion Mills, Llango,
Gwent NP5 4TJ
Tel: 01594 53100

ARMSTRONG WORLD INDUSTRIES LTD
PVC- and cushion-backed sheet
Fleck Way, Teesside Industrial Estate,
Thornaby TS17 9JT
Tel: 0800 371849

F BALL AND CO LTD
Wide range of adhesives
Churnetside Business Park,
Cheddleton, Staffs ST13 7RS
Tel: 01538 361633

BRINTONS CARPETS
Carpet manufacturers
PO Box 16, Exchange Street,
Kidderminster, Worcs DY10 1AG
Tel: 01562 820000

CAMPBELL MARSON & CO LTD
Hardwood flooring systems
Unit 34, Wimbledon Business Centre,
Riverside Road, London SW17 0BA
Tel: 0181 879 1909

CONTRACT FLOORING ASSOC.
Advice on laying and contractors
4c St. Mary's Place, The Lace Market,
Nottingham NG1 1PH
Tel: 0115 941 1126

CRAFT COUNCIL
Index of rug makers and mosaic artists
44a Pentonville Road, Islington,
London N1 9BY
Tel: 0171 278 7700

CRUCIAL TRADING
Natural fibres
Pukka Palace, 174 Tower Bridge Road,
London SE1 5OD
Tel: 0171 234 0000

CUSTOM CARPET CO. LTD
Bespoke carpet manufacturer
50 Dymock Street, Fulham
London SW6 3HA
TEL: 0171 736 3338

DALSOUPLE DIRECT LTD
Rubber flooring
PO Box 140, Bridgewater,
Somerset TA5 1HT
Tel: 01278 733133

DOMUS TILES
Supply and lay ceramics and mosaic
33 Parkgate Road,
Battersea, London SW11 4NP
Tel: 0171 223 5555

DURABELLA LTD
Sound reducing floor systems
Eastways Industrial Estate,
Withan, Essex CM8 3YQ
Tel: 01376 517345

ECOMAX ACOUSTICS
Sound reducing floor systems
Gomm Road, High Wycombe,
Bucks HP13 7DJ
Tel: 01494 436345

EGETAEPPER (UK) LTD
Artist design wool rugs and fitted carpets
Ege House, Chorley North Business Park,
Drumhead Road, Chorley, Lancs, PR6 7BL
Tel: 01257 239000

CHRISTOPHER FARR
Contemporary rugs
115 Regents Park Road,
London NW1 8UR
Tel: 0171 916 7690

FIRED EARTH
Hard flooring, natural fibres and rugs
Twyford Mill, Oxford Road,
Adderbury, Nr. Banbury,
Oxon OX17 3HP
Tel: 01295 812088

FOCUS CERAMICS
Supply and lay tiles, stone and mosaic
Unit 4, Hamm Moor Lane,
Weybridge, Surrey, KT15 2SD
Tel: 01932 854 881

FORBO NAIRN LTD
Linoleum, vinyl and cushion-backed sheet
PO Box 1, Kircaldy, Fife KY1 2SB
Tel: 01592 643777

GOODING ALUMINIUM LTD
Aluminium flooring
1 British Wharf, Landmann Way
London SE14 5RS
Tel: 0181 692 2255

DAVID GUNTON HARDWOOD
FLOORING
Decorative hardwood floors
Grange Lane, White Gate,
Winsford, Cheshire CW7 2P
Tel: 01606 861442

JOSEPH HAMILTON & SEATON LTD.
Synthetic haircord carpet
JHS House, Gerard,
Lichfield Road Industrial Estate,
Tamworth, Staffs B79 7UW
Tel: 01827 311102

HEUGA CARPET TILES
Carpet tiles and other textured flooring
Interface Europe Ltd
Ashlyns Hall, Chesham Road
Berkhamsted, Herts HP4 2ST
Tel: 01442 285000

INTERNATIONAL PAINT PLC
Paint and varnish manufacturers
Stoneygate Lane, Felling-on-Tyne,
Gateshead, Tyne and Wear NE10 0JY
Tel: 0191 469 6111

JAYMART RUBBER AND PLASTICS LTD
*Rubber sheet, and range of mats
and stair accessories*
Woodlands Trading Estate, Eden Vale
Road, Westbury, Wilts BA13 3QS
Tel: 01373 864926

H & R JOHNSON
Tile manufacturer
Highgate Tile Works, Tunstall,
Stoke on Trent, Staffs ST6 4JX
Tel: 01782 575575

JUNCKERS LTD
Wood floor systems
Wheaton Court Commercial Centre,
Wheaton Road, Wiltham,
Essex CM8 3UJ
Tel: 01376 517512

THE KILIM WAREHOUSE
Kilims
28a Pickets Street
London SW12 8QB
Tel: 0181 675 3122

KIRKSTONE QUARRIES
British and imported slates
Skelwith Bridge, Ambleside,
Cumbria LA22 9NN
Tel: 015394 33296

LASAR EUROPE LTD
Specialist in floor coatings
Woodlands Business Park, Rougham
Industrial Estate, Bury St. Edmunds,
Suffolk IP30 9ND
Tel: 01395 271417

LASSCO
Salvaged materials
Architectural Flooring (London) Ltd,
The Vicarage, Market Street,
London EC2A 4ER
Tel: 0171 739 0448

**CHRISTOPHER LEGGE
ORIENTAL CARPETS**
Oriental carpets
Oakthorpe Road, Summertown
Oxford OX2 7BD
Tel: 01865 557572

JOHN LEWIS GROUP
Carpet and other flooring
Oxford Street, London W1A 1EX
Tel: 0171 629 7711

LIFE ENHANCING TILE CO
Encaustic tile manufacturers
31 Bath Buildings, Montpelier
Bristol BS6 5PT
Tel: 0117 907 7673

LIBERON WAXES LTD
Wood finishing products
Mountfield Industrial Estate,
Learoyd Road, New Romsey,
Kent TN28 8XU
Tel: 01797 367 555

MARBLE FLOORING SPECIALIST LTD
Supply and lay marble
110 Ashley Down Road, Bristol, BS7 9JR
Tel: 0117 942 0221

HARVEY MARIA LTD
PVC and laminated cork tiles
17 Mysore Road, London SW11 5RY
Tel: 0171 350 1964

MOSAIC WORKSHOP
Mosaic workshop
Unit B, 443-449 Holloway Road,
London N7 6LJ
Tel: 0171 263 2997

NATURAL COATINGS CO.
Wood finishes
Unit 5A, Tonedale Industrial Estate,
Milverton Road, Wellington, TA21 0AA
Tel: 01823 664859

NATURAL FLOORING DIRECT
Natural fibres
Unit A02 Tower Bridge Business Complex,
St. Clements Road,
London SE16 4DJ
Tel: 0800 454721

NATURESTONE
Supply and lay lime, sandstone and slate
Crossways, London Road,
Ascot, Berks, SL5 0PZ
Tel: 01344 27617

ROGER OATES DESIGN ASSOCIATES
Wide range design rugs and natural flooring
The Long Barn, Eastnor, Ledbury,
Herefordshire HR8 1EL
Tel: 01531 632718

ORIGINAL STYLE
Reproduction Victorian tiles
Falcon Road, Sowton Industrial Estate,
Exeter, Devon EX2 7LF
Tel: 01392 474011

PARIS CERAMICS
Supply and lay wide range of hard flooring
583 Kings Road, London SW6 2EH
Tel: 0171 371 7778

PISANI MARBLE COMPANY
Marble, granite and stone
Transport Avenue, Great West Road,
Brentford TW8 9HF
Tel: 0181 568 5001

RELICS OF WITNEY
Wood finishing products and tuition
35 Bridge Street, Witney, Oxon OX8 6DA
Tel: 01993 704611

DENIS RUABON LTD
Manufacture quarry tiles
Hafod Tileries, Ruabon,
Wrexham, Clwyd LL14 6ET
Tel: 01978 843484

SOURCES

SADOLIN (UK) LTD
Wood-finish products
Sadolin House, Meadow Lane,
St. Ives, Cambridgeshire PE17 4UY
Tel: 01408 496868

SINCLAIR TILL
Carpet, natural, hardwood and sheet flooring
791-793 Wandsworth Road
London SW8 3JQ
Tel: 0171 720 0031

SOMER UK
Linoleum, vinyl and artificial carpet
Berry Hill Industrial Estate, Droitwich,
Worcs WR9 9AB
Tel: 01905 795004

STONE AGE
Supply and lay lime- and sandstone
19 Filmer Road, London SW6 7BU
Tel: 0171 385 7954

STONE FEDERATION OF GREAT
BRITAIN
Names of suppliers and installers
82 New Cavendish Street,
London W1M 8AD
Tel: 0171 580 5588

STONELL LTD
Natural stone, limestone, slate, sandstone
Bockingfold, Ladham Road,
Goudhurst, Kent TN17 1LY
Tel: 01580 211167

TAKE LTD
Japanese tatami mats
14-15 New College Parade,
London NW3 5EP
Tel: 0171 586 0064

TARKETT
*Natural wood and composite
vinyl-faced wood system*
Poyle House, PO Box 173, Blackthorn
Road, Colnbrook SL3 0AZ
Tel: 01753 684533

TIMBMET
Timber supplier
PO Box 39, Chawley Works,
Cumnor Hill, Oxford OX2 9PP
Tel: 01865 862223

BRUNO TRIPLET LTD
*Contemporary furnishing textiles,
woodtwine and twisted linen matting*
First floor, Chelsea Harbour Design Centre,
London SW10 0XE
Tel: 0171 795 0395

THE TURTLE MAT COMPANY
Washable cotton doormats
92a Kings Road
Kingston
Surrey KT2 5HT
Tel: 0181 541 0569

VIGERS HARDWOOD FLOORING
SYSTEMS LTD
Supply and lay hardwood floor systems
Beechfield Walk, off Seward Stone Road,
Waltham Abbey, Essex EN9 1AY
Tel: 01992 711133

WATCO (SALES) LTD
Concrete and cement coatings and repairs
Watco House, Filmer Grove,
Godalming, Surrey GU7 3AL
Tel: 01483 425000

WORLDS END TILES
Supply wide range of tiling
British Rail Yard, Silverthorne Road,
Battersea, London SW8 3HE
Tel: 0171 720 1435

YORK HANDMADE BRICK CO
Brick suppliers
Forest Lane, Alne, York YO6 2LU
Tel: 01347 838881

AUSTRALIA

ADVANCE FLOORING
*Parquetry specialists, timber, cork and
floating floors*
'The Old Bakery', 33 Alexandra Street,
Hunters Hill NSW 2110
Tel: (02) 9879 6555

ADVANCE FLOORING
Parquetry, timber flooring
71-73 Belmain Street, Richmond
Vic 3121
Tel: (03) 9427 1822

CANBERRA CARPET CHOICES
Carpets, cork tiles, vinyl, parquetry
Cnr Lathlain and Cohen Streets,
Belconnen Town Centre,
Belconnen ACT 2617
Tel: (06) 251 2913

CARPET CALL PTY LTD
Rugs, parquetry, vinyl, timber, cork, carpet
2 Village Court, Mulgrave Vic 3170
Tel: (03) 9561 6333

CARPET CALL PTY LTD
*Timber flooring, ceramics, parquetry,
cork, carpet*
45 The Parade, Norward SA 5067
Tel: 1300 369 469

CARPET CALL PTY LTD
Rugs, parquetry, vinyl, timber, cork, carpet
6 Dividend Street, Mansfield Qld 4122
Tel: (07) 3343 7800

EDWARDS SLATE AND TILE
Slate, sandstone, terracotta, limestone
12 Lionel Road, Mount Waverley
Vic 3149
Tel: (03) 9544 9544

KINGSTON FLOOR COVERING
CENTRE
Carpets, vinyls, ceramic tiles, rugs, cork
Mertonvale Circuit, Kingston Tas 7050
Tel: (03) 6229 7700

MR CARPET (SALES) PTY LTD
Parquetry, cork, carpet, vinyl, rugs
358 Eastern Valley Way,
Chatswood NSW 2067
Tel: (02) 9417 8800

PALLOS CARPET CHOICES
Carpet, vinyl, cork
1500 Albany Highway,
Shop 3, Cannington WA 6107
Tel: (09) 356 5577

SOLOMONS
Carpets, vinyl, cork, parquetry
37 Pickering Street, Alderley Qld 4051
Tel: (07) 3354 1544

CANADA

ACCURATE FLOOR FASHIONS
*Carpet, linoleum, hardwoods, ceramic
and marble tile*
105 West Second Avenue,
Vancouver, British Columbia V5Y 1B8
Tel: 604 879 3848

ACTIVE MARBLE AND TILE
Granite, marble, slate and agglomerates
31 Skyline Crescent NE,
Calgary, Alberta T2K 5X2
Tel: 403 274 2111

ALLAN RUG CO LTD
Wool and sisal
2120 Eglinton Ave West,
Toronto, Ontario M6E 2K6
Tel: 416 787 1707

ATELIER SU MESURA
Marble and granite
11320 Nicolas Josselin, Montreal,
Quebec H1E 3A2
Tel: 514 881 0469

CALEDONIA MARBLE CO LTD
Marble and granite tiles
167 Bentworth, Toronto,
Ontario M6A 1P6
Tel: 416 782 6568

CARPET BAGGERS
Carpet, vinyl, ceramic and marble tile
9 – 2016 25th Ave NE, Calgary,
Alberta T2E 6Z4
Tel: 403 250 9097

GUILDCRAFT FLOORS
*Selection of broadloom, vinyl, tile,
hardwood and ceramic*
702 Weston Road, Toronto,
Ontario M6N 3P4
Tel: 416 769 4154

JORDAN'S CARPETS
Carpet, vinyl, ceramic and hardwood
5055 Calgary Trail N Bound,
Edmonton, Alberta T6H 4R7
Tel: 403 435 3794

JORDAN'S CARPETS
Carpet, vinyl, ceramic, hardwood
1470 West Broadway, Vancouver,
British Columbia V5N 1V8
Tel: 604 733 1174

PARADISE CARPETS
*Carpet, linoleum, hardwood, ceramic tile,
marble*
3651 – 99 Street, Edmonton,
Alberta T6E 6K5
Tel: 403 437 1957

LES TAPIS ROSA
Carpets, ceramic stone and glass
109 Cure Poirier, Longueuil,
Quebec J4J 2G2
Tel: 514 463 3752

TRI-CAN CONTRACTING
Custom carpet and vinyl, tile
81 Milvan Drive, Toronto,
Ontario M9L 1Y8
Tel: 416 741 0849

WESTERN FLOORING
*Carpet, linoleum, ceramic, tile, hardwood
and granite*
3806 A Macleod Trail SE,
Calgary, Alberta T2G 5B6
Tel: 403 243 4526

Bibliography

The following books give a general overview of design considerations and some of the materials covered. In the majority of cases details of composition and performance can best be obtained from manufacturers' catalogues, which are also the best source of specific instructions for laying, treating and maintaining each floor material.

Austwick, J., *The Decorated Tile*, Pitman House, London, 1980
Barnard, J., *Victorian Ceramic Tiles*, Studio Vista, London, 1972
Barnard, N., Hull, A., Merrell, J., *Living with Kelims*, Thames and Hudson, London, 1996
Bloomer, Carolyn M., *Principles of Visual Perception*, The Herbert Press, London, 1990
Bridgeman, R., *Weaving – A Manual of Techniques*, The Crowood Press, Wiltshire, 1991
Friends of the Earth, *Good Wood Guide*, London, 1997
Gilbert, C., Lomax, J., and Wells-Cole, A., *Country House Floors*,
    Leeds City Art Gallery, 1987
Gombrich, E.H., *The Sense of Order*, Phaidon, Oxford, 1984
Goodwin, Arthur, *The Technique of Mosaic*, Batsford, London, 1985
Haack, H., *Oriental Rugs*, Faber & Faber, London, 1960
Hamilton, D., *Architectural Ceramics*, Thames and Hudson, London, 1979
Holloway, D., and Milson, F., *Floors and Tiles – Letts Home Decorator*,
    New Holland, London, 1996
Hosker, Ian, *Complete Woodfinishing*, Guild of Master Craftsman Publications, Lewes 1993
Howarth, Maggie, *The Art of Pebble Mosaics*, Search Press, Tunbridge Wells, 1996
Innes, Jocasta, *The New Paint Magic*, Frances Lincoln, London, 1992
Pearson, D., *The Natural House Book*, Conran Octopus, London, 1991
Vance, P., and Goodrick-Clarke, C., *The Mosaic Book*, Conran Octopus, London, 1994
Van Lemmen, Hans, *Tiles in Architecture*, Laurence King, London, 1993
Wagstaff, Liz, *Paint Recipe Book*, Quadrille Publishing/Country Living, London, 1995
Yagi, Koji, *A Japanese Touch for Your Home*, Kodansha International, New York, 1991
For anyone seeking a survey of historic design details of floors and all other building
    elements, a most useful reference work is:
Calloway, S. (ed.), *The Elements of Style*, Mitchell Beazley, London, 1996

Index

INDEX

Author's Acknowledgments

When I accepted Frances Lincoln's invitation to write the text I had no idea what a pleasure it would be: thanks first to Frances for believing I might be up to the task and for her quiet encouragement; thanks also to the editorial team who never let the rigour required to deliver the book spoil my enjoyment of the process. The book owes a great deal, as do I, to Sally Cracknell – no author could wish for a more talented, perceptive and co-operative designer.

My colleagues at Berman Guedes Stretton Architects, 25 Cave Street, Oxford OX4 1B and Thomas Rayson Partnership accommodated my very irregular work pattern and provided constructive comment; Simon Norris made a valuable contribution to Wood. It was a pleasure to talk about materials with the people who produce and work them and who take a craftsman's delight in the quality and technicalities of materials and workmanship. To the following I am grateful for the time they took to impart some of their knowledge and to check the text: Liz Fecitt at Kirkstone Quarries, Mike Hardiman at Brintons Carpets, Richard O'Grady at Stone Age, and Costas Sakellarios at Pisani Ltd. Thanks to the following for reading the text and providing essential corrections – any errors or shortcomings remain my own: Emma Biggs at Mosaic Workshop, Piero Cassandro of Domus Tiles, Janet Green of Crucial Trading, David Gunton of David Gunton Hardwood Flooring, Robert Handy of Timbmet, Steve Witt of Jaymart Ltd, David Muncey of Forbo Nairn and mosiacist Anna Wyner. Greatest thanks of all go to the home team of Phillipa, Zoe and particularly Alison for continuous encouragement and support and for accepting with such tolerance and humour the chaos I brought into our home.

Publishers' Acknowledgments

Frances Lincoln Publishers would like to thank James Bennett, Hilary Mandleberg and Peggy Vance for their initial work on the book; Ruth Carim for proofreading; Kathie Gill for the index; Sara Robin for design assistance; and Amanda Patton for the artwork.

Editors   Caroline Bugler, Christine O'Brien
Art Editor   Sally Cracknell
Editorial Assistant   Sarah Labovitch
Picture Researcher   Sue Gladstone
Production Controller   Liz Stewart
Art Director   Caroline Hillier
Editorial Director   Erica Hunningher
Head of Pictures   Anne Fraser

Photographer's Acknowledgments

a=above, *b*=below, *c*=centre, *l*=left, *r*=right *D*=designer, *A*=architect

1 John Ferro Sims; 2-3 René Stoeltie (Karen Cheryl, *D* Fréderic Méchiche); 5 The Life Enhancing Tile Company; 6 Deidi von Schaewen (*A* Jim Rossant, New York); 7 Deidi von Schaewen; 8 Simon Kenny/*Belle*/Arcaid; 9 Deidi von Schaewen (Mr & Mrs Armand Bartos, *A* Claudio Silverstrin); 10-11 Paris Ceramics; 14 Ray Main; 15 Peter Woloszynski/The Interior Archive Ltd.; 17 Julie Phipps/Arcaid; 18*a* Deidi von Schaewen; 18*b* Jean-Pierre Godeaut; 19 Fritz von der Schulenburg/The Interior Archive Ltd.; 20 Fritz von der Schulenburg/The Interior Archive Ltd. (*A* Andrea Taverner); 21 Ianthe Ruthven (Nicolas Groves-Paines, Kristin Hannesdottir); 22 Peter Woloszynski/The Interior Archive Ltd.; 23 Deidi von Schaewen (Kathleen Warren); 24-25 Ray Main; 26-27 James Mortimer/The Interior Archive Ltd. (*D* Jacques Grange); 27*a* Paris Ceramics; 28 Robert Franklin Architects, Oxford (Tel:01865 311440); 29 Stonell Ltd.; 31 Andreas von Einsiedel (*D* Fréderic Méchiche); 32 Nadia Mackenzie (Joseph Ettedgui); 33 John Ferro Sims; 34 Julie Phipps/Arcaid; 35*a+c* Fired Earth; 35*b* Stonell Ltd.; 36-37 Fritz von der Schulenburg/The Interior Archive Ltd. (*A* Nico Rensch); 38 *The World of Interiors*/Thibault Jeanson (*D* Stephen Sills & James Huniford); 39*a+c* Fired Earth; 39*b* Simon Kenny/*Vogue Living*; 40 John Ferro Sims; 41 John Hall; 42-43 Roberto Polidori; 44 Alberto Piovano/Arcaid (*A* Cecillia & Ottorino Berselli); 45 Deidi von Schaewen (Mr & Mrs Armand Bartos, *A* Claudio Silverstrin); 46-47 Paul Ryan/International Interiors (M. Kreigel); 47*a* The Life Enhancing Tile Company; 48 John Ferro Sims; 49*a* Fritz von der Schulenburg/The Interior Archive Ltd. (*D* Mimmi O'Connell); 49*b* Paris Ceramics; 50 René Stoeltie (*D* Fréderic Méchiche); 51*a,c+bl* Fired Earth; 51*br* Andreas von Einsiedel (*D* Monika Apponyi); 52 Bernard Touillon/*Côté Sud*/Elizabeth Whiting and Associates; 53 Fritz von der Schulenburg/The Interior Archive Ltd. (*D* Mimmi O'Connell); 54 Cecilia Innes/The Interior Archive Ltd.; 55 Deidi von Schaewen (*D* Christian Astuguevielle); 56 The Life Enhancing Tile Company (*D* Robert Manners); 57 Fritz von der Schulenburg/The Interior Archive Ltd. (*D* Rima El-Said); 58-59 Polly Farquharson (*D* Sebastian Fisher); 60 Christopher Simon Sykes/The Interior Archive Ltd. (Maxine de la Falaise); 61 Fritz von der Schulenburg/The Interior Archive Ltd. (*A* Paula Navone); 62 Verne; 63-64 Deidi von Schaewen; 65 Jacques Dirand/The Interior Archive Ltd. (Gerard Decoster); 66*a* Domus Tiles Limited; 66-67 Massimo Listri; 68 Philip H. Ennis Photography (*D* Terra Designs); 69*a* Domus Tiles Ltd; 69*b* Simon Kenny/*Vogue Living*; 70 Paris Ceramics; 71*al+cl* Paris Ceramics; 71*ar* Ray Main; 71*cr* Domus Tiles Ltd.; 71*bl* Nadia Mackenzie; 71*br* John Ferro Sims; 72 John Ferro Sims; 73*l* Domus Tiles Ltd.; 73*r* Jean-Pierre Godeaut; 74*l* Fritz von der Schulenburg/The Interior Archive Ltd. (*A* Paula Navone);

74*r* David Churchill/Arcaid; 75 Andreas von Einsiedel (*D* Tatiana von Hesser); 76 Nadia Mackenzie; 77 Jean-Pierre Godeaut (*D* Martine Lionel Dupont); 78-79 Junckers Ltd.; 79*a*, 80-81 Campbell Marson & Co.Ltd.; 83 Jan Verlinde (*D* Pieter Vandenhout); 84 Simon Kenny/*Vogue Living*; 85 Robin Mathews; 86*l* Alberto Piovano/Arcaid (*A* P. Robbrecht); 86*r* Junckers; 87 Deidi von Schaewen (M. Torreciliat); 88 Andreas von Einsiedel (*D* Axel Vervoordt); 89 Sinclair Till; 90-91 *Elle Decoration*; 92 René Stoeltie (*D* Fréderic Méchiche); 93 John Hall; 94 Henry Wilson/The Interior Archive Ltd. (Celia Lyttleton); 95 *The World of Interiors*/Jacques Dirand; 96 Jan Tham/*Sköna Hem*/Camera Press; 97 *The World of Interiors*/Henry Bourne; 98 Tom Leighton/Elizabeth Whiting and Associates; 99 Richard Bryant/Arcaid (*A* Gwathmey Siegel) 100*a* Brintons; 100-101 Andreas von Einsiedel (*D* Ina Lindemann); 102 Ege Axminster A/S (Fischbild, 1925); 103 Fritz von der Schulenburg/The Interior Archive Ltd. (*D* Mimmi O'Connell); 104 Fritz von der Schulenburg/The Interior Archive Ltd.; 105*a* John Ferro Sims; 105*b* Christopher Farr (*D* Allegra Hicks); 107 Deidi von Schaewen; 108*a,c+br* Brintons; 109 Interface Europe Ltd.; 110 Verne; 111 Fritz von der Schulenburg/The Interior Archive Ltd. (*D* Mimmi O'Connell); 112 John Hall; 114*a* Jean-Pierre Godeaut (Jacques Damaze); 114*b* Rob Gray (*D* Christine Van der Hurd of CVDH Design) 114-115 Deidi von Schaewen (*D* Christian Duc); 116 Nadia Mackenzie (*D* Anta Scotland Ltd.); 117 Jonathan Pilkington/The Interior Archive Ltd.; 118 Jan Baldwin (Roger Oates Design Associates); 119 Andreas von Einsiedel (*A* John Simpson); 120-121 Nadia Mackenzie; 122*a* Crucial Trading; 122-123 Alan Weintraub/Speranza /Arcaid (*D* Orlando Diaz-Azcuy); 124 Andreas von Einsiedel (*D* Tatiana von Hessen); 125 Fritz von der Schulenburg/The Interior Archive Ltd. (*D* Richard Mudditt); 126-128 Crucial Trading; 129+130*l* Tim Clinch/The Interior Archive Ltd.; 130-131 Christopher Simon Sykes/The Interior Archive Ltd.; 132 Bruno Triplet Ltd.; 133 David Parmiter; 134 Andreas von Einsiedel (*D* Monika Apponyi); 135 Roger Oates Design Associates; 137 Lars Hallen (Isotalo); 138*a* Sinclair Till; 138-139 Georgia Glynn Smith (Sinclair Till); 141 Sinclair Till; 142 Ray Main; 143*al* Sinclair Till; 143*ar+b* Jonathan Pilkington/The Interior Archive Ltd.(*A* Justin Meath-Baker); 144-145 Simon Upton/*Homes & Gardens*/Robert Harding Picture Library; 146 Ray Main; 147 Fritz von der Schulenburg/The Interior Archive Ltd. (Andre Heller); 148*a,cl+br* Amtico; 148*cr+bl* Harvey Maria Ltd.; 150*a* Altro Floors; 150*ac,bc+b* Jaymart Rubber & Plastics Ltd.; 151 Wicanders 152-153 Henry Wilson/The Interior Archive Ltd. (*D* Sophie Saren); 154-155 Jason Lowe © Condé Nast PL *House and Garden*; 156*a* Gooding Aluminium; 156-157 Sandro Sodano; 158 Reiner Blunck/Arcaid (*A* Mark Mack); 159 John Edward Linden/Avanti Architects Ltd. (*D* Justin de Syllas); 160 Andreas von Einsiedel (*D* Charles Rutherfoord); 161 Gooding Aluminium; 162 Ray Main; 163 *The World of Interiors*/ James Mortimer; 164 Jean-Pierre Godeaut; 165 Richard Bryant/Arcaid (*A* John Young); 166 Bill Amberg; 167 Lasar Europe Ltd.; 168-169 Simon Brown/The Interior Archive Ltd. (Michael Casey); 169*a* Sinclair Till